Is your head in the clouds dreaming of the perfect interior as a background for your wonderful life? We hope so, and this can apply to anyone anywhere, to young and old alike. 'Ah, be practical', say the sensible ones. But there is no time limit on dreams: patience is the answer and then practicality can combine with inspiration.

So once again this catalog, the fifth of its kind, attempts not only to give you the most romantic ideas imaginable, but to offer help and encouragement in making them reality. Needless to say, if dreams do not appeal there are some very down to earth ideas as well.

'Too many castles in the air' we were reprimanded after last year's photographs. So we found the newest, smallest house in London to prove that even that can be just as much fun, especially as we chose brilliantly coloured fabrics and a black and white tiled floor ready for dancing.

The billiard room was a last ditch attempt at eccentricity and came about because another location fell through. 'How many people have billiard rooms' was the inevitable stern rebuke. But really it is just such a perfect room for its purposes.

The little marquee (for taking lunch when the weather is inclement) turned out to look so adorable in its tropical green and white that the pundits were rendered speechless and had to nod a weak assent.

Then, because it was time we showed an American house, we went to Long Island, and there before our eyes stood this very friendly house waiting for us. A perfect example of the Federal period of architecture, the house itself was so charming that it really was not very difficult at all to decorate it to look utterly beautiful.

Back to Wales, our good old roots as it were, for some down to earth stuff. A real artist's studio came first, housed in a very practical cottage, and then simple bedrooms in classic sprig designs. And in a lovely Georgian house in the Welsh mountains we decorated the breakfast room for viewing the breathtaking sunrise. Then naturally we had to include a very traditonal bedroom full of country roses, as our own favourite environment for waking up in the country.

Lastly our favourite picture of all: a formal Rococo dining room furnished with blue damask lined with pink (printed of course). Looking incredibly grand it's a triumph of what can be done by you yourself, with inspiration, patience and in this case the use of a colour forgotten for nearly two centuries.

Laura Ashley

INDEX

INTRODUCTION TO ROOM SETS

On the following 52 pages are to be found photographs and descriptions of nineteen rooms, entirely decorated with the wallpaper, fabrics and accessories featured in this catalog. In order to demonstrate the versatility of the collection the rooms have been selected from a number of houses deliberately chosen for their diversity of style and period.

A brief description of each house or room is followed by hints on choice of decoration, an analysis of the methods and materials used, and a summary of the effect created. Each room set is followed by a photograph of the major prints used in its decoration, together with other fabrics and wallpapers and a selection of products, to show how the collection has been designed to fully co-ordinate.

Hopefully these examples will suggest ways in which various products may be combined to suit your own particular purposes, so that armed with the detailed information given in the second half of the catalog, you will find it a simple and enjoyable exercise to co-ordinate the decoration of any room, or even an entire house.

BEDROOM

The essential thing to remember when planning the decoration of any bedroom is that it should be comfortable, with an atmosphere of luxurious tranquility in which one can relax completely and forget the worries of the day. Such an environment can be created quite easily with a little imagination and the correct choice of fabrics and paint.

Particularly suitable for a bedroom, although they may be used to great effect in more formal rooms, are large floral prints in warm shades of pink and red. The first step in decorating this bedroom in an English country house was to colour wash the walls a soft rose pink; a clever and effective variation on the use of a basic and inexpensive decorating material.
This quiet background colour forms the perfect base for a typically English late Victorian design of huge cabbage roses on a delicate trellis ground, trimmed with bright red, on the curtains, the drapes of the half tester bed, quilt and cushions. Their softly swirling contours in subtly gradiated tones of pink and green seem to rise out of the fabric and fill the room, combining with the smaller rosebud print on the sofa and valance, and a trailing rose garland border, to transform this bedroom into a peaceful, floral bower.

Walls:
Soft Rose, Vinyl Matt Emulsion Paint Wash.

Wallpaper Border:
F627, Rose Multi White.

Bed-hanging, Quilts, Cushions & Curtains in Drawing Room Fabric:
Country Roses, Rose Multi White.

Bed-hanging Lining, Valance, Cushions, Sofa & Stool in Country Furnishing Cotton:
Rosamund, Rose Multi White.

Coolie Lampshade:
Rose.

Column Lampbase:
Rose/White.

ENGLISH COUNTRY HOUSE

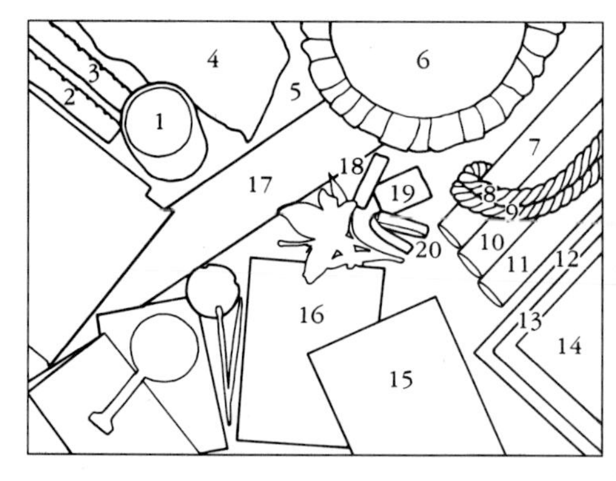

1. Emulsion Paint **Soft Rose**
2. Fringing **Rose**
3. Fringing **Moss**
4. Country Furnishing Cotton **Clover** Rose/White
5. Lace Panel **White**
6. Frilled Cushion **Kate** Rose/Moss/White
7. Wallpaper **Wickerwork** Rose/White
8. Tie-back **Moss**
9. Tie-back **Rose**
10. Wallpaper **Palmetto** Rose/Moss/White
11. Wallpaper **Candy Stripe** Rose/White
12. Country Furnishing Cotton **Wickerwork** White/Rose
13. Country Furnishing Cotton **Candy Stripe** Rose/White
14. Country Furnishing Cotton **Palmetto** Rose/Moss/White
15. Country Furnishing Cotton **Rosamund** Rose Multi White
16. Drawing Room Fabric **Country Roses** Rose Multi White
17. Wallpaper Border F627 Rose Multi White
18. Braid **Rose/Moss/White**
19. Fabric Border F510 Rose Multi White
20. Plain Gimp **Moss**

ARTIST'S STUDIO, COUNTRY COTTAGE

In the heart of the Black Mountains lies this tiny cottage, used for many years by an artist as a country retreat. The decor is chosen with great care since it must attempt the impossible, being restrained enough to allow the artist to work creatively, but at the same time producing the necessary variety to give the house a definite personality.

The colour chosen for the walls of the studio was a light apricot, cleverly applied over a coat of white emulsion, leaving minor brush strokes to give a slightly textured appearance. The finished tone is sufficiently light to display the pictures hung on it to the best effect, yet warm enough to give the room a highly individual character. Many colours co-ordinate well with this versatile base colour to produce a number of very different effects. In this case, curtains and cushions are in a striking contemporary print, inspired by the sophisticated palette and swirling patterns of English avant-garde artists of the early twentieth century.

Its wild brush strokes, splashes and blots accentuated by a cream ground, blend perfectly with the pale walls and simple limed floorboards to inject just the right amount of artistic excitement into this simple rural interior.

Walls:
Soft Apricot, Vinyl Matt Emulsion Paint.

Curtains & Cushions in Country Furnishing Cotton:
Emma, Multi Straw Cream.

HEREFORDSHIRE, ENGLAND

1. Piped Cushion **Rose**
2. Piped Cushion **Aquamarine**
3. Piped Cushion **Emma** Multi Straw Cream
4. Piped Cushion **Sapphire**
5. Ceramic Tiles **Pavilion** Rose/White
6. Ceramic Tiles **Wickerwork** Rose/White
7. Country Furnishing Cotton **Emma** Multi Guava Stone
8. Wallpaper **Sophie** Multi Straw Cream
9. Emulsion Paint **Soft Rose**
10. Emulsion Paint **Light Guava**
11. Gloss Paint **Apricot**
12. Emulsion Paint **Stone**
13. Emulsion Paint **Light Aquamarine**

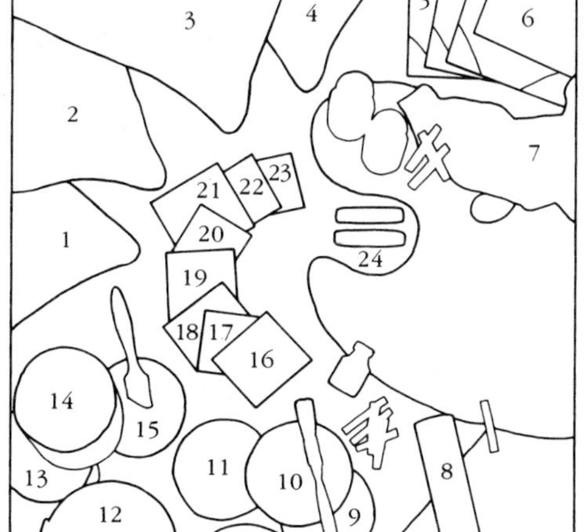

14. Gloss Paint **Plum**
15. Emulsion Paint **Sapphire**
16. Country Furnishing Cotton **Candy Stripe** Rose/White
17. Country Furnishing Cotton **Candy Stripe** Sapphire/White
18. Country Furnishing Cotton **Sapphire**
19. Country Furnishing Cotton **Regatta** Sapphire/White
20. Country Furnishing Cotton **Brighton Rock** Sugar Pink/White
21. Wallpaper **Brighton Rock** Sugar Pink/White
22. Wallpaper **Candy Stripe** Rose/White
23. Wallpaper **Candy Stripe** Sapphire/White
24. Plain Gimp **Sapphire & Rose**

MRS. BOURDILLON'S BREAKFAST ROOM

Traditionally, the breakfast room is not only a place in which to eat, but an informal sitting room in which members of the family can gather at any time in relaxed surroundings. To create the appropriate atmosphere demands a form of decoration far less ornate than that of a more conventional dining room. Here, such an effect has been achieved using, for curtains, cushions and chairs, an attractive large floral print in pinks, greens, smokey blues and browns, whose origins lie in parochial English country houses of the 1820's, and which would not seem out of place in a more formal environment. A delicate design of stylised pink tulips on a stippled ground of cool mint green for the banquettes, acts as a foil to the larger botanical print, picking up the light which floods the large bay window, and, with the pale tones of the woodwork, carrying the green of the hills into the room to give the feeling of a fresh spring morning. The diagonal symmetry of the tulips complements that of the room itself, in which any tedious regularity is defeated by the random placing in the master print of a variety of large and

WELSH COUNTRY HOUSE

colourful flowers, thus ensuring the required atmosphere of charmingly simple and comfortable informality.

Curtains, Cushions & Upholstery in Drawing Room Fabric:
Kew Gardens, Mint Multi White.

Blinds & Banquettes in Country Furnishing Cotton:
Penelope, Mint Multi White.

1. Drawing Room Fabric **Kew Gardens** Mint Multi White
2. Frilled Cushion **Penelope** Mint Multi White
3. Plain Gimp & Fringing **Aquamarine** & Fringing **Rose**
4. Country Furnishing Cotton **Salon** Rose/Candy
5. Country Furnishing Cotton **Salon** Mint/Aquamarine
6. Piped Cushions **Aquamarine & Rose**
7. Frilled Cushion **Kew Gardens** Mint Multi White
8. Wallpaper **Candy Stripe** Rose/White
9. Wallpaper **Wickerwork** Rose/White
10. Wallpaper **Salon** Rose/Candy
11. Wallpaper **Penelope** Mint Multi White
12. Wallpaper **Trellis** Sand/White
13. Wallpaper **Salon** Sand/White
14. Wallpaper **Wickerwork** White/Sand
15. Wallpaper **Salon** Mint/Aquamarine
16. Emulsion Paint **Light Aquamarine**
17. Gloss Paint **Rose**
18. Tie-back **Aquamarine**

DINING ROOM

Argueably the most formal and serious room of any house is the dining room. As it is here that entertainment is at its most civilised the decoration should present a sense of order, while at the same time remaining intimate enough to make it a pleasant place in which to relax over lunch or dinner.

This dining room in a small Georgian country house is an excellent example of what can be achieved with relatively little difficulty and few materials when restoring a room to its original style. The ceiling has been painted pale cream and the walls a subtle smoke blue, taken up in the ground of the print used on the curtains and upholstery. This copy of an original 18th century damask, with its classic design in two tones of blue, gives a feeling of richness to the room, particularly when combined with a flamboyant rose pink lining and fringe.

The overall effect, so simply achieved, is of a gracious splendour quite formal enough for the smartest dinner party, yet in its simple colour scheme totally lacking in pretension.

Curtains & Upholstery in Country Furnishing Cotton: **Damask**, Kingfisher/Smoke.

Curtain Lining in Country Furnishing Cotton: **Rose**.

GEORGIAN HOUSE, BERKSHIRE, ENGLAND

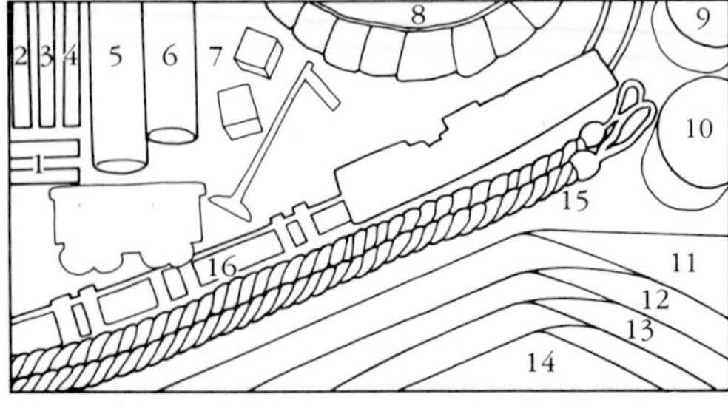

1
2
3
4
5
6
7
8
9
10
11
12
13
14
15
16

1. Plain Gimp **Smoke & Rose**
2. Braid **Kingfisher/Smoke**
3. Braid **Plum/Saddle/Cream**
4. Braid **Smoke/Cream**
5. Wallpaper **Damask** Kingfisher/Smoke
6. Wallpaper **Louis** Kingfisher Multi Stone
7. Country Furnishing Cotton **Damask** Kingfisher/Smoke
8. Frilled Cushion **Paisley** Smoke/Kingfisher/Cream
9. Emulsion Paint **Light Smoke**
10. Emulsion Paint **Stone**
11. Country Furnishing Cotton **Gingham** Kingfisher Multi Cream
12. Country Furnishing Cotton **Rose**
13. Country Furnishing Cotton **Paisley** Smoke/Kingfisher/Cream
14. Country Furnishing Cotton **Grapes** Smoke Multi Cream
15. Tie-back **Rose**
16. Tie-back **Smoke**

GARDEN PAVILION

CHATEAU IN PICARDY, FRANCE

A languid summer afternoon whiled away in the heart of the countryside. In the evening one might dine outside under an elegant striped awning. The air is heavy with the scent of summer flowers. Cool, crisp formal green and white stripes reflect the gentle mood, while a delicate lily of the valley print echoes the lavish bouquet spiralling above.

Pavilion & Tablecloth in Country Furnishing Cotton:
Marquee, Tropical Green/ White.

Lining in Chintz:
Lily of the Valley, Tropical Green Multi Stone.

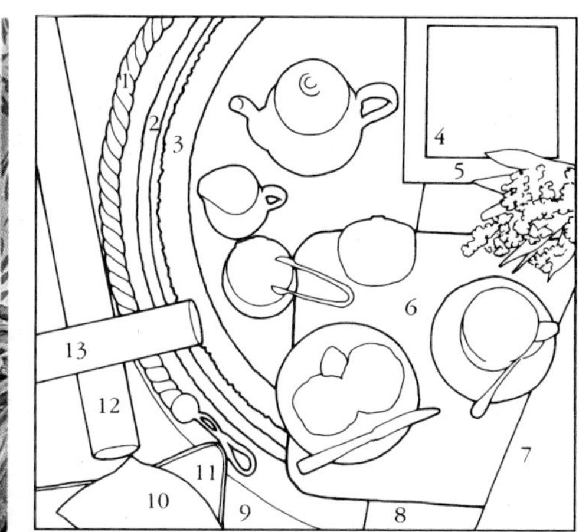

1. Tie-back **Tropical Green**
2. Plain Gimp **Tropical Green**
3. Fringing **Tropical Green**
4. Ceramic Tile **Conservatory** Leaf Green/White
5. Ceramic Tile **Trellis** Apple/White
6. Dining Collection **Nutmeg** White/Moss
7. Country Furnishing Cotton **Marquee** Tropical Green/White
8. Country Furnishing Cotton **Conservatory** Leaf Green/White
9. Country Furnishing Cotton **Tropical Green**
10. Chintz **Lily of the Valley** Tropical Green Multi Stone
11. Piped Cushion **Tropical Green**
12. Wallpaper **Trellis** Apple/White
13. Wallpaper **Marquee** Tropical Green/White

ATTIC BEDROOM

The decoration of an attic bedroom is a perfect example of how to make the most of a small, confined space. One should avoid any dark colours, heavy designs and too much elaborate detail, which would almost certainly leave the room feeling dull and claustrophobic. Instead, delicate prints with light backgrounds should be used with a lot of white, to reflect and disperse the light and so brighten the room.

These basic principles have been successfully applied to this tiny bedroom in a Welsh country cottage, producing impressive results with as little expense as possible.

The low ceiling has been made to look higher by being given a few coats of the same ordinary white emulsion paint applied to the old bedstead, fireplace and pelmet.

The walls have been pushed out with the use of a light, simple, Regency print of twining branches and posies of violet and bright cherry, which was universally popular throughout the nineteenth century. Curtains and a bedspread in the same colours on a delicately stippled ground co-ordinate easily, ensuring the feeling of space found in this refreshingly simple, delightfully feminine bedroom.

COUNTRY COTTAGE, WALES

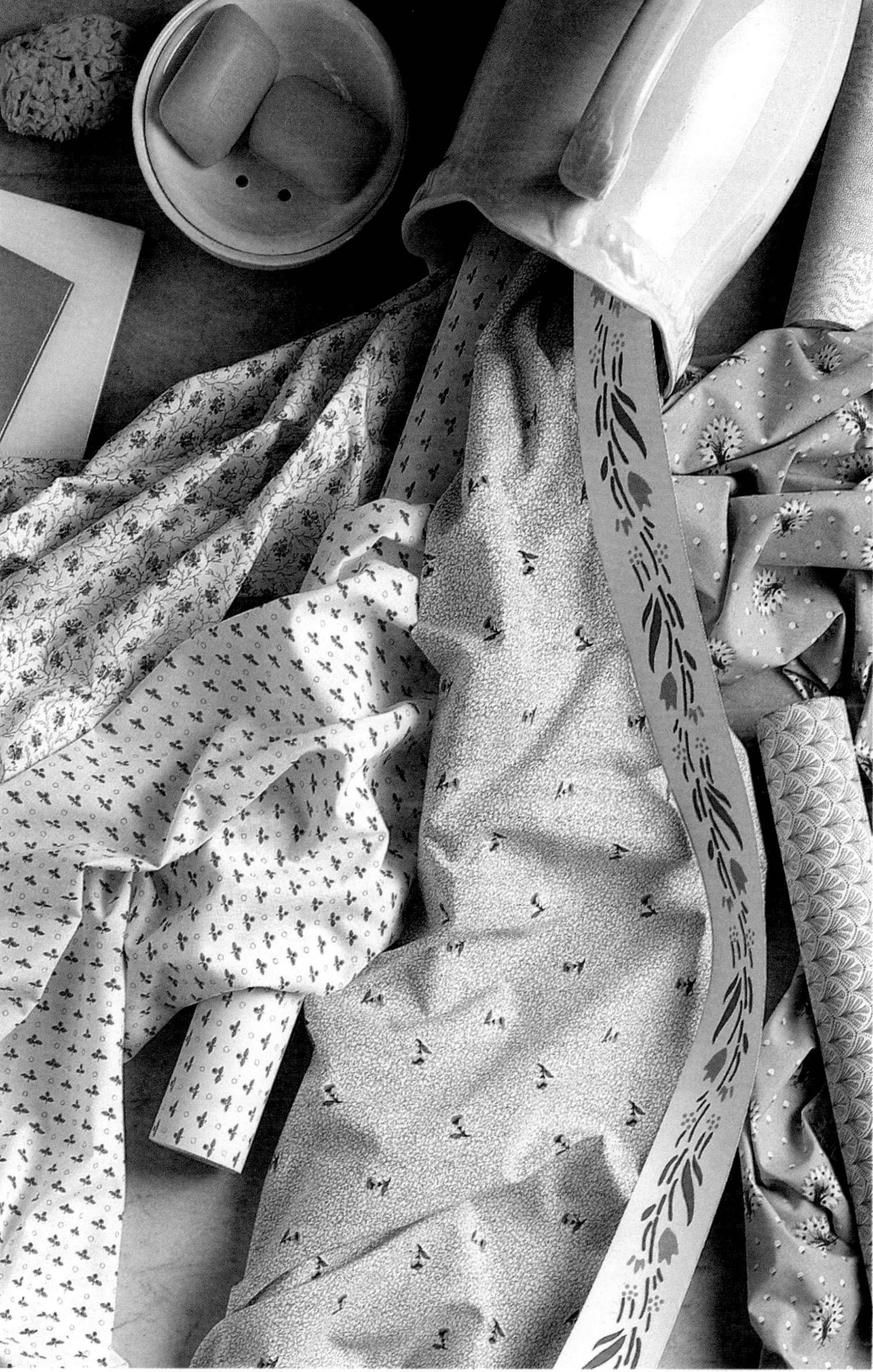

Wallpaper:
Imogen, Cherry Multi White.

Curtains in Country Furnishing Cotton:
Harriet, Cherry Multi White.

Valance & Quilt Lining
in Country Furnishing Cotton:
Imogen, Cherry Multi White.

Pillow & Quilt in Country Furnishing Cotton:
Harriet, Cherry Multi White.

Towels: **White**.

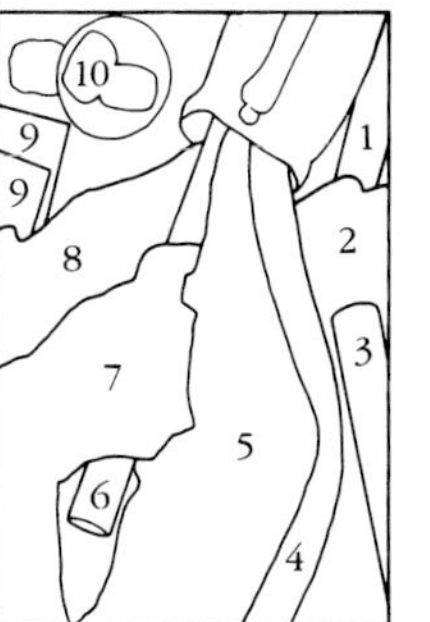

1. Wallpaper **Parapet** Taupe/White
2. Country Furnishing Cotton **Pondicherry** Light Sage Multi White
3. Wallpaper **Palmetto** Dark Green/Raspberry/Sand
4. Wallpaper Border L631 Rose/Moss/White
5. Country Furnishing Cotton **Harriet** Cherry Multi White
6. Wallpaper **Polly** Cherry Multi White
7. Country Furnishing Cotton **Polly** Cherry Multi White
8. Country Furnishing Cotton **Imogen** Cherry Multi White
9. Ceramic Tiles **Rose & White**
10. Large Round **Soap Dish & Soap**

SEASIDE HUT

SUSSEX COAST, ENGLAND

In a tiny seaside house, the sitting room is usually the centre of family life. Although a certain amount of formal order is needed, the atmosphere should essentially be cheerful and unfussy, encouraging relaxed, informal conversation.
Here an eighteenth century chintz of intertwining roses and pansies has been combined with a pink and white candy stripe wallpaper which serves to give the room a certain formality.

The bright pink picks up the floral tones of the chintz, which, complemented by the pale sapphire blue found on the tablecloths and lamp, provides the overall image.
Two old wicker chairs have been given new life with a coat of white gloss paint and colourful chintz cushions, while co-ordinating plain scatter cushions, comfortably strewn about, complete the light pastel shades of this charmingly versatile room.

Wallpaper:
Brighton Rock, Sugar Pink/White.

Tablecloth in Country Furnishing Cotton:
Regatta, Sapphire/White.

Chairs in Chintz:
English Garden, Taupe Multi White.

Piped Cushions:
Sapphire, **Rose** & **Aquamarine**.

Coolie Lampshade:
Sapphire.

Column Lampbase:
Sapphire/White.

LIVING ROOM, CONTEMPORARY TOWN HOUSE

LONDON

Furnishing a contemporary dwelling often imposes troublesome spatial limitations upon the interior decorator. In this house, these problems have been overcome by the use of bold geometric patterns and primary colours. The walls and ceiling were painted plain white, and the window hangings kept deliberately light to allow furnishings and floor design alone to define space. The floor is tiled in such a way that an expanse of white is broken up by interesting squares of sharply contrasting black. This overall lack of colour opens up the room, setting the scene for the striking primaries used for the upholstery, door hangings and tablecloth. These three colours, denim blue, bright poppy and tropical green complement each other perfectly, and in their broad stripes and bold blocks of colour, provide sufficient interest for the entire room. The striking simplicity of this scheme is well shown in the entrance hall, where a simple inexpensive black and white wallpaper border applied to a white-painted wall creates an instant effect. The living room itself is divided into two distinct functional areas by a large oriental carpet, while a simple and stylish dining table has been created by draping a large geometrically patterned tablecloth in two of the primary colours over a red cloth on a basic table structure.

As a whole, this arrangement provides an attractive example of an economical and efficient way of furnishing any contemporary house.

Walls:
White, Vinyl Matt Emulsion Paint.

Curtains in Country Furnishing Cotton:
Marquee, Tropical Green/White.

Blind in Country Furnishing Cotton:
Tropical Green.

Large Ceramic Tiles:
Pavilion, Black/White.

Chairs, Sofa, Settle & Door Hanging in Country Furnishing Cotton:
Henley, Denim Multi White.

Small Square Tablecloth:
Harlequin, Denim/Tropical Green/White.

Tablecloth in Country Furnishing Cotton:
Poppy.

Piped Cushions:
Poppy & **Columbine**, Denim Multi White.

Coolie Shade with matching column base:
Tropical Green.

Walls:
White, Vinyl Matt Emulsion Paint.

Wallpaper Border:
F594, Black/White.

Large Ceramic Tiles:
Pavilion, Black/White.

1. Piped Cushion **Poppy**
2. Small Square Tablecloth **Harlequin** Denim/Tropical Green/White
3. Country Furnishing Cotton **Marquee** Tropical Green/White
4. Wallpaper Border F594 Black/White
5. Country Furnishing Cotton **Nutmeg** White/China Blue
6. Ceramic Tiles **Pavilion** Black/White
7. Wallpaper **Dandelion** Denim/Tropical Green/White
8. Wallpaper **Cricket Stripe** Sapphire/China Blue/White

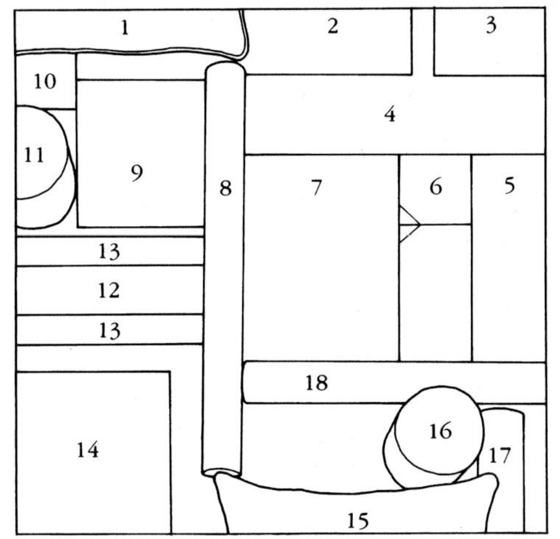

9. Ceramic Tile **Domino** Denim/White
10. Chintz **Tropical Green**
11. Gloss Paint **China Blue**
12. Fabric Border F368 Demin Multi White
13. Plain Gimp **Sapphire & Moss**
14. Country Furnishing Cotton **Henley** Denim Multi White
15. Cushion **Columbine** Denim Multi White
16. Gloss Paint **Poppy**
17. Wallpaper **Marquee** Tropical Green/White
18. Wallpaper **Cottage Sprig** China Blue/Moss/White

BILLIARD ROOM

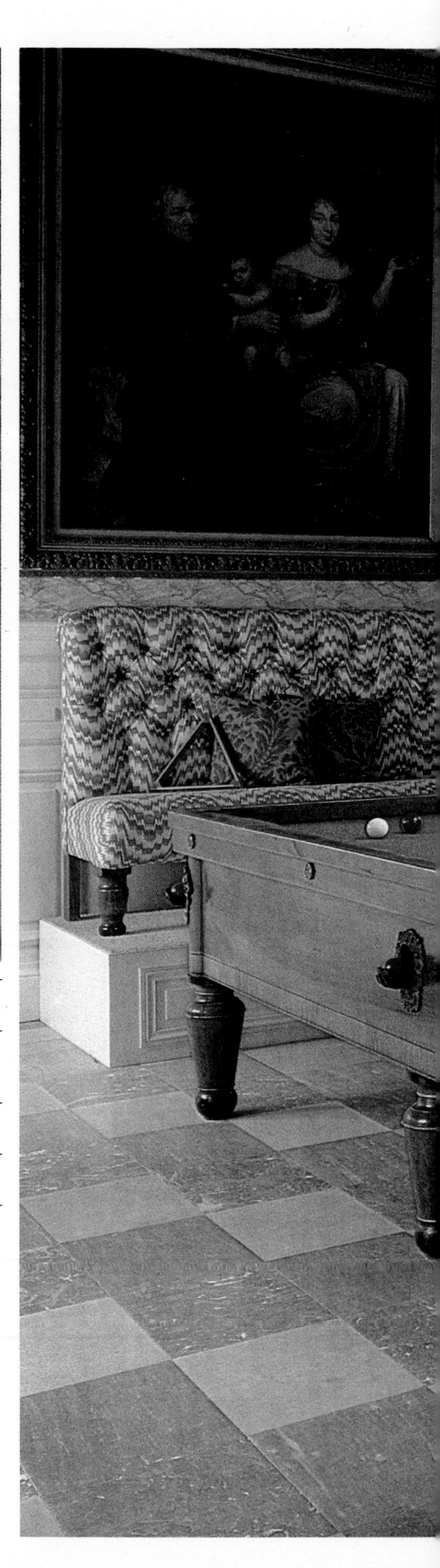

The original function of this billiard room in the eighteenth century was as a 'Salle de Chasse', the room in which the huntsmen of the estate would gather to display their prizes after the chase.

Today this room is still largely the closely guarded territory of the male members of the family, as can be seen in the decoration, which displays certain distinctly masculine qualities. The regularity of the trompe l'oeil faux marble wallpaper acts as a restrained background to the more dramatic traditional green flamestitch found on the benches, and co-ordinates perfectly with the dark green damask print of the curtains and cushions.

As a whole the room presents an extremely sober, orderly and unfussy atmosphere, which could never interfere with the mood of civilised informality always to be found here.

Wallpaper:
Marble, Greengage Multi Stone.

Curtains & Cushions in Country Furnishing Cotton:
Damask, Dark Green/Mid Green.

Settles in Drawing Room Fabric:
Florentina, Dark Green Multi Stone.

Cushions in Country Furnishing Cotton:
Moss.

CHATEAU IN PICARDY, FRANCE

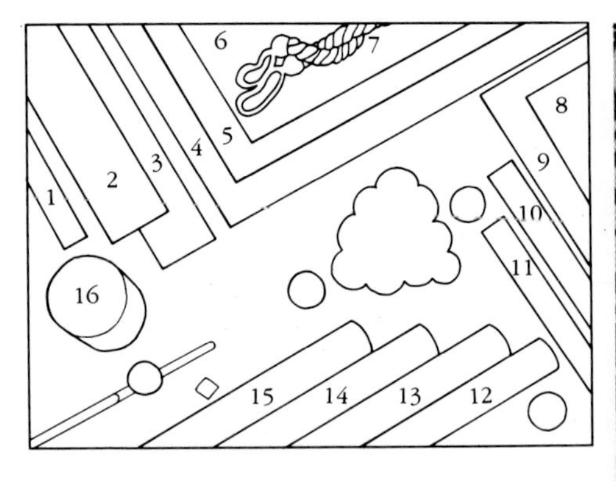

1. Braid **Dark Green/Burgundy/Sand**
2. Wallpaper Border F539 Sand/Dark Green
3. Wallpaper Border F539 Sand/Burgundy
4. Drawing Room Fabric **Florentina** Dark Green Multi Stone
5. Country Furnishing Cotton **Palmetto** Dark Green/Raspberry/Sand
6. Country Furnishing Cotton **Damask** Dark Green/Mid Green
7. Tie-backs **Burgundy & Moss**
8. Drawing Room Fabric **Favorita** Dark Green Multi Sand
9. Country Furnishing Cotton **Blazer Stripe** Coriander/Burgundy
10. Braid **Sage**
11. Plain Gimp **Burgundy**
12. Wallpaper **Marble** Greengage Multi Stone
13. Wallpaper **Palmetto** Dark Green/Raspberry/Sand
14. Wallpaper **Nutmeg** Sage/Cream
15. Wallpaper **Wickerwork** Sage/Cream
16. Emulsion Paint **Light Sage**

FARMHOUSE BEDROOM

The decoration of this small bedroom in a Welsh farmhouse called for a light and delicate approach. Since wallpaper alone would have lacked sufficient definition, a simple paper border, in a mid-nineteenth century print of a colourful floral bouquet, was used with a co-ordinating wallpaper print of cherry flowers with light green leaves on a white ground. The bed, covered with a co-ordinating combination of these two prints, and hung with a voluminous drape of white voile suspended from a simply constructed corona, has the appearance of a comfortable, early nineteenth century day bed.

The use of such a simple hanging in voile, cotton or chintz can completely transform the most ordinary of bedrooms, immediately making them appear softer and more hospitable. This farmhouse bedroom now exudes all the romantic association of the Regency era, without being at all pretentious, or having lost any of its simple rural charm.

Wallpaper:
Polly, Cherry Multi White.

Wallpaper Border:
F591, Deep Sapphire Multi White.

Quilt in Country Furnishing Cotton:
Morning Parlour, Cherry Multi White.

Pillows & Quilt Lining in Country Furnishing Cotton:
Polly, Cherry Multi White.

RADNOR, WALES

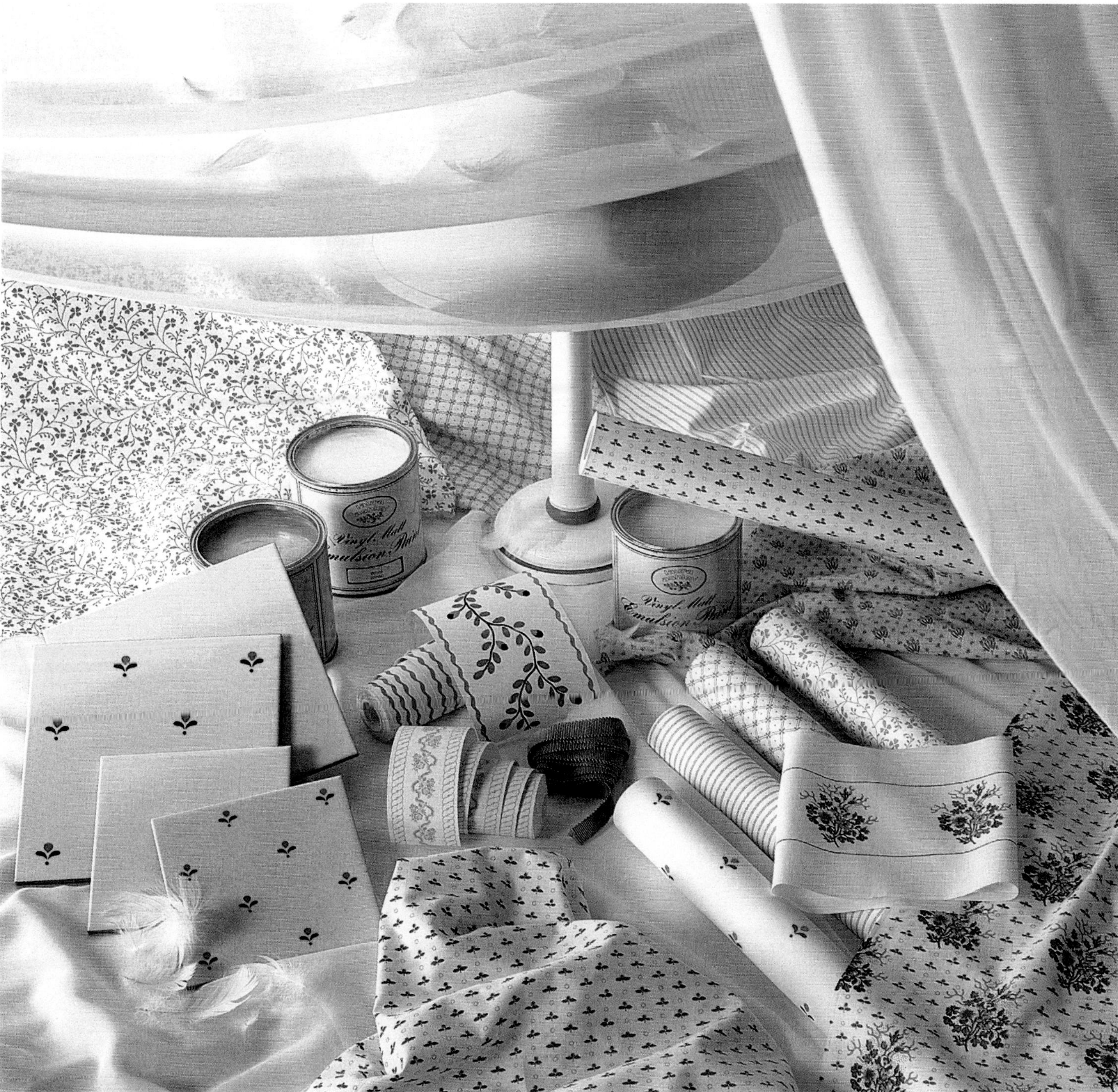

1. Column Lampbase **Sapphire/White**
2. Coolie Lampshade **Sapphire**
3. Country Furnishing Cotton **Candy Stripe** Sapphire/White
4. Country Furnishing Cotton **Poona** Leaf Green/Raspberry/White
5. Wallpaper **Polly** Cherry Multi White
6. Country Furnishing Cotton **Morning Parlour** Sapphire Multi White
7. Fabric Border F591 Deep Sapphire Multi White
8. Wallpaper **Campion** Sapphire/White
9. Wallpaper **Wickerwork** Sapphire/White
10. Wallpaper **Candy Stripe** Sapphire/White

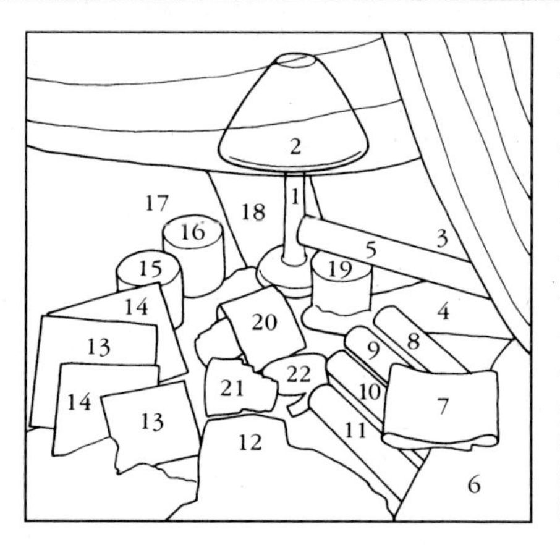

11. Wallpaper **Bembridge** Sapphire/Mid Blue/White
12. Country Furnishing Cotton **Polly** Cherry Multi White
13. Ceramic Tiles **Bembridge** Sapphire/Mid Blue/White
14. Ceramic Tiles **White**
15. Emulsion Paint **Soft Sapphire**
16. Emulsion Paint **White**
17. Country Furnishing Cotton **Campion** Sapphire/White
18. Country Furnishing Cotton **Wickerwork** Sapphire/White
19. Emulsion Paint **Soft Rose**
20. Wallpaper Border P897 Sapphire/Moss/White
21. Wallpaper Border T210 Rose/White
22. Plain Gimp **Sapphire**

ENTRANCE HALL

COUNTRY HOUSE, WALES

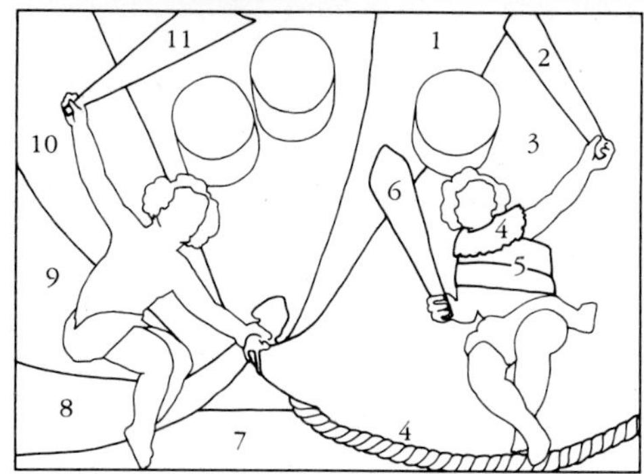

1. Wallpaper **Albert** Oak Multi Sand
2. Wallpaper **Wickerwork** Sage/Cream
3. Country Furnishing Cotton **Grapes** Smoke Multi Cream
4. Plain Gimp **Sapphire**, Fringing **Navy** & Tie-back **Smoke**
5. Braids **Smoke/Cream** & **Kingfisher/Smoke**
6. Wallpaper **Nutmeg** Saddle/Sand
7. Wallpaper Border F539 Cloud Blue/Oak
8. Country Furnishing Cotton **Petite Fleur** Cream/Smoke
9. Country Furnishing Cotton **Paisley** Smoke/Kingfisher/Cream
10. Country Furnishing Cotton **Damask** Kingfisher/Smoke
11. Wallpaper **Trellis** Sand/Cream

The entrance hall is one of the most important rooms in any house, greeting the visitor with an immediate statement about the character of the host. For this reason, its decoration and furnishings should attempt to express as much as possible about the taste and lifestyle of the owner. The modest entrance hall of this Welsh country house has been decorated with a subtle colour scheme of smoke blue, oak brown and sand to produce a feeling of warmth which envelops any newcomer and welcomes him into the house. The sense of regularity which defines the confined space is achieved with a combination of two designs based on prints by the important nineteenth century designer, Owen Jones: a Gothic revival trellis wallpaper and classical acanthus leaf border, always so effective against a block of plain colour. As well as being treated as a prelude to the rest of the house, the decoration of an entrance hall should be planned bearing in mind the frequency with which it is used. In order to cope with the demands of muddy boots, dogs and children, it must be hard-wearing, and not too light in colour. The colour scheme used here satisfies both these purposes. While the oak brown is dark enough to cope with any muddy pawmarks, blue and sand provide the necessary levity to give the scheme a convivial, welcoming atmosphere.

Wallpaper:
Albert, Oak Multi Sand.

Wallpaper Border:
F539, Cloud Blue/Oak

SUSSEX DOWNS, ENGLAND

Picnics are a traditional part of an English Summer. Whether with smoked salmon and champagne in a punt on the Cam, or chocolate cake, cherries and cider on the rolling Sussex Downs, they always go more smoothly when given a little forethought.

Everyone knows how much a pleasant environment can add to the enjoyment of a lunch or dinner party, and often a great deal of time and effort is put into the decoration of a dining room. Why should the same principle not be applied to a picnic, harmonising all the paraphernalia of outdoor eating with the surrounding countryside?

Here a traditional red gingham check has been used for a tablecloth with matching napkins. Large, comfortable cushions are covered in a strikingly bold print of huge yellow poppies on a bright red ground, and the light and cheerful atmosphere is completed with place-mats and a tea-cosy in a pretty red and white sprig design.
These brilliant primaries work well with one another, perfectly complementing the surrounding colours of the countryside in high summer, and turning an ordinary picnic into a special occasion.

Tablecloth & Napkins:
Gingham, Poppy Multi White.

Place-mats, Tea-cosy & Egg-cosies:
Cottage Sprig, Poppy/Apple/White.

Cushions in Country Furnishing Cotton:
Summertime, Multi Poppy.

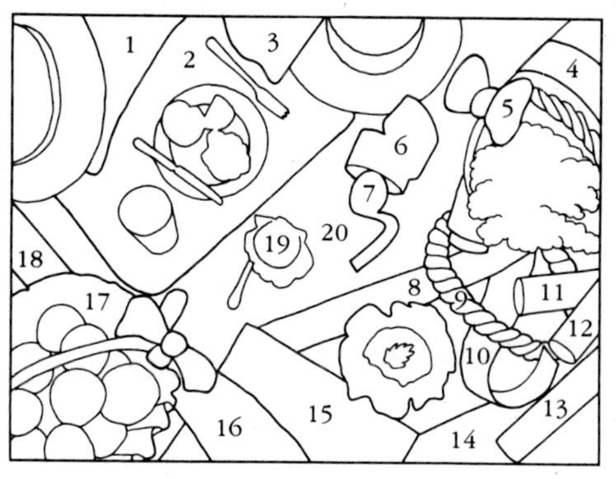

1. Piped Cushion **Poppy**
2. Place-mat **Cottage Sprig** Poppy/Apple/White
3. Napkin **Gingham** Poppy Multi White
4. Fabric Border F46 Mustard Multi White
5. Fabric Border L631 Poppy/Apple/White
6. Wallpaper Border F46 Mustard Multi White
7. Plain Gimp **Poppy**
8. Wallpaper Border F46 Poppy Multi White
9. Tie-back **Poppy**
10. Wallpaper Border L631 Poppy/Apple/White
11. Wallpaper **Wood Violet** Mustard/Apple/White
12. Wallpaper **Trellis** Mustard/White
13. Wallpaper **Cottage Sprig** Poppy/Apple/White
14. Country Furnishing Cotton **Midsummer** Mustard Multi White
15. Country Furnishing Cotton **Summertime** Multi Poppy
16. Fabric Border F46 Poppy Multi White
17. Country Furnishing Cotton **Floribunda** Multi Poppy
18. Wallpaper **Trefoil** White/Mustard
19. Country Furnishing Cotton **Trefoil** White/Mustard
20. Country Furnishing Cotton **Gingham** Poppy Multi White

PROVENCAL HALL

The warm southern sun of Provence casts deep shadows on the terracotta tiles and flagstones of farmhouse and château. Inside all is cool tranquility.

A delicate print of wild flowers in warm reds, blues and yellows can fill a room with colour and light. The soft background tone of golden ochre gently blends with the quiet yellows, greys and browns which give this region its unique feeling of rustic charm.

A tiny red diamond design on a beige ground completes this picture of simple French provincial style, which demonstrates perfectly how to use formal prints in an informal setting without appearing at all affected.

Wallpaper, Curtain & Tablecloth in Country Furnishing Cotton:
Indienne, Multi All-Spice.

Upholstery & Napkins in Country Furnishing Cotton:
Simla, Multi All-Spice.

Upholstery Trim:
Burgundy, Plain Gimp.

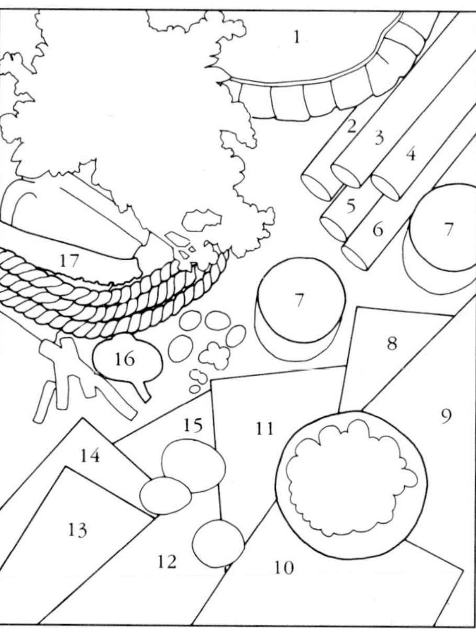

1. Frilled Cushion **Paisley** Plum/Saddle/Cream
2. Wallpaper **Simla** Multi All-Spice
3. Wallpaper **Stipple** Apricot/Primrose
4. Wallpaper **Wickerwork** Sage/Cream
5. Wallpaper **Nutmeg** Saddle/Sand
6. Wallpaper **Infinity** Smoke/Cream
7. Emulsion Paint **Soft Rose** & **Light Sage**
8. Country Furnishing Cotton **Pondicherry** Light Sage Multi White
9. Country Furnishing Cotton **Indienne** Multi All-Spice
10. Country Furnishing Cotton **Rawalpindi** Multi Cinnamon
11. Drawing Room Fabric **Florentina** Burgundy Multi Stone
12. Country Furnishing Cotton **Simla** Multi All-Spice
13. Country Furnishing Cotton **Palmetto** Dark Green/Raspberry/Sand
14. Country Furnishing Cotton **Nutmeg** Cream/Sage
15. Country Furnishing Cotton **Wickerwork** Cream/Sage
16. Braid & Gimp **Burgundy**, **Kingfisher/Smoke**, **Sapphire Sage**, **Smoke/Cream** & **Dark Green/Burgundy/Sand**
17. Fringing & Tie-backs **Rose**, **Burgundy** & **Smoke**

DRAWING ROOM, GEORGIAN HOUSE

The classical proportions of this eighteenth century drawing room are perfectly suited to the pale elegance of the colours with which it has been decorated. The painted panelling, highlighted in two different tones of the same colour, blends happily with the soft apricot chintz of the swagged curtains, lined in pale aquamarine and edged with a slightly darker co-ordinating fringe.

Two sofas, upholstered in a light aquamarine chintz with apricot piping, the direct reverse of the colour scheme found on the curtains, have been arranged around the focal point of the elaborate marble fireplace to provide a comfortable sitting area. These pale tones are perfect for an English summer. In winter the sofas might have loose covers in a deeper hue, or a bold pattern of swirling vines and flowers. Cushions in pale apricot, rose and aquamarine chintzes, and fresh, bright floral prints, with co-ordinating lampshades complete the tranquil atmosphere of this light summer drawing room.

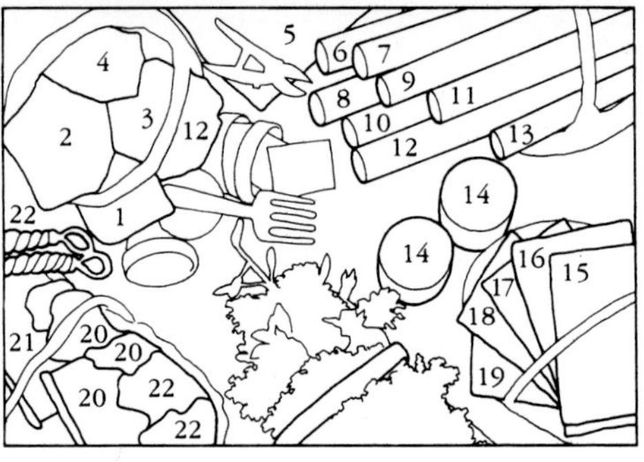

Curtains in Chintz:
Apricot.

Fringing & Tie-backs on Curtains:
Aquamarine.

Sofas in Chintz:
Aquamarine, with Apricot Piping.

Square Frilled Cushion:
Kew Gardens, Mint Multi White.

Round Frilled Cushions:
Penelope, Mint Multi White.

Piped Cushions:
Rose, **Apricot** & **Aquamarine**.

Tablecloth in Chintz:
Aquamarine.

Coolie Shade with matching column base:
Rose.

1. Chintz **Aquamarine**
2. Country Furnishing Cotton **Regency Stripe** Aquamarine/Apricot/White
3. Country Furnishing Cotton **Penelope** Mint Multi White
4. Country Furnishing Cotton **Salon** Mint/Aquamarine
5. Country Furnishing Cotton **Regency Stripe** Apricot/Aquamarine/White
6. Wallpaper **Regency Stripe** Aquamarine/Apricot/White
7. Wallpaper **Trellis** Apricot/Apricot Wash
8. Wallpaper **Salon** Apricot/Apricot Wash
9. Wallpaper **Floribunda** Multi Apricot
10. Wallpaper **Bindweed** Multi Apricot
11. Wallpaper **Regency Stripe** Apricot/Aquamarine/White
12. Wallpaper and Country Furnishing Cotton **Palmetto** Aquamarine/Apricot/White
13. Wallpaper **Penelope** Mint Multi White
14. Emulsion Paint **Light Aquamarine & Soft Apricot**
15. Country Furnishing Cotton **Palmetto** Apricot/Aquamarine/Apricot Wash
16. Chintz **Apricot**
17. Country Furnishing Cotton **Bindweed** Multi Apricot
18. Country Furnishing Cotton **Salon** Apricot/Apricot Wash
19. Country Furnishing Cotton **Floribunda** Multi Apricot
20. Plain Gimp **Apricot, Rose, & Aquamarine**
21. Braid **Aquamarine/Apricot**
22. Fringing & Tie-backs **Aquamarine & Apricot**

BERKSHIRE, ENGLAND

ENTRANCE HALL, 19TH CENTURY HOUSE

This square-built house on Long Island in the Greek Revival manner, originally the home of a retired sea-captain, has been completely restored to its original American Federal style. This type of decoration, the first attempt by post-Revolutionary Americans to create a national style, was popular from the establishment of the first Federal Government in 1789, until about 1830. Essentially it consists of a new world austerity with English overtones of Robert Adam and early Regency. Decoration is basic, naïve and sometimes even primitive in its simplicity, but always displays an innate sense of style. This small entrance hall characterises the overall feel of the house. Wallpaper in a tiny blue and cream print gives an impression of stippled paint, providing more interest than would a simple coat of emulsion, yet still in keeping with the original atmosphere.

Wallpaper:
Infinity, Smoke/Cream.

SAG HARBOUR, NEW YORK

1. Country Furnishing Cotton **Cordelia** Multi Stone
2. Wallpaper **Petite Fleur** Terracotta/Cream
3. Wallpaper **Shepherd's Purse** Smoke/Cream
4. Wallpaper Border F539 Cloud Blue/Oak
5. Wallpaper **Wild Clematis** Cream/Smoke
6. Wallpaper Border T210 Smoke/Cream
7. Wallpaper **Wild Clematis** Smoke/Cream
8. Wallpaper **Wickerwork** Sage/Cream
9. Wallpaper **Nutmeg** Sage/Cream
10. Wallpaper **Infinity** Smoke/Cream
11. Wallpaper **Tulips** Multi Stone

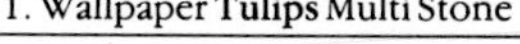

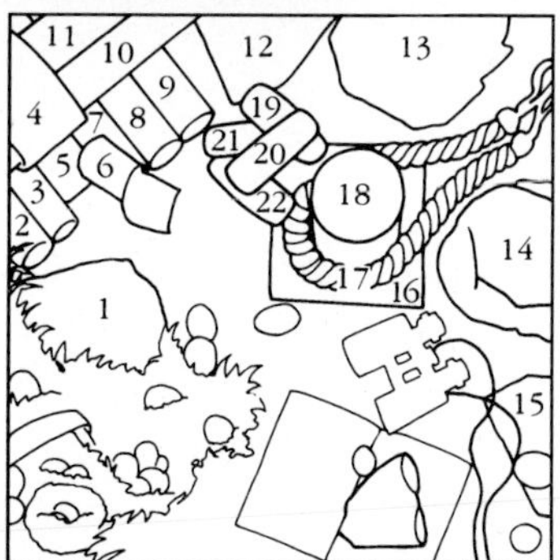

12. Country Furnishing Cotton **Wild Clematis** Cream/Smoke
13. Country Furnishing Cotton **Tulips** Multi Stone
14. Country Furnishing Cotton **Wickerwork** Cream/Sage
15. Country Furnishing Cotton **Petite Fleur** Cream/Smoke
16. Ceramic Tile **White**
17. Tie-back **Smoke**
18. Emulsion Paint **Light Smoke**
19. Braid **Smoke/Cream**
20. Plain Gimp **Terracotta**
21. Plain Gimp **Smoke**
22. Braid **Sage**

FRONT PARLOUR

Although essentially a formal room, the predominating feeling of the front parlour is of relaxed simplicity. The walls are softened by a stippled wallpaper in restful shades of apricot, similar to that used in the hall, confined by a border of stylised leaves in blue and sand found in a sample book of borders in a museum library, and closely resembling the stencils in popular use during the Federal period.

The print used on the curtains, sofa and cushions is adapted and enlarged from an early nineteenth century design found on a patchwork quilt. Its charmingly naïve likenesses of poppies and cornflowers in pale rustic colours close to those of the original vegetable dyes, make it ideal for a country sitting room.

Wallpaper, border and fabric co-ordinate in perfect harmony, and, together with the simple limed fireplace and scrubbed floor, and a splash of contrast from the salmon armchair, establish the appropriate mood of comfortable austerity.

Wallpaper:
Stipple, Apricot/Primrose.

Wallpaper Border:
F510, Smoke Multi Stone.

Sofa, Curtains & Cushions in Country Furnishing Cotton:
Cordelia, Multi Stone.

Armchair in Country Furnishing Cotton:
Delhi, Multi Salmon.

Cushion in Country Furnishing Cotton:
Rawalpindi, Multi Cinnamon.

Cushion in Country Furnishing Cotton:
Paisley, Smoke/Kingfisher/Cream.

19TH CENTURY HOUSE, SAG HARBOUR, NEW YORK

1. Frilled Cushion **Sea Spray** Kingfisher/Stone
2. Country Furnishing Cotton **Gingham** Kingfisher Multi Cream
3. Country Furnishing Cotton **Wild Clematis** Cream/Smoke
4. Country Furnishing Cotton **Paisley** Smoke/Kingfisher/Cream
5. Country Furnishing Cotton **Petite Fleur** Cream/Smoke
6. Country Furnishing Cotton **Wild Cherry** Cream/Smoke
7. Country Furnishing Cotton **Cordelia** Multi Stone
8. Country Furnishing Cotton **Wickerwork** Cream/Sage
9. Country Furnishing Cotton **Stipple** Apricot/Primrose
10. Country Furnishing Cotton **Nutmeg** Cream/Sage
11. Plain Gimp **Sage**
12. Plain Gimp **Smoke**
13. Wallpaper **Edward** Kingfisher/Stone
14. Wallpaper **Wild Cherry** Smoke/Cream
15. Wallpaper **Infinity** Smoke/Cream
16. Wallpaper **Petite Fleur** Smoke/Cream
17. Wallpaper **Nutmeg** Sage/Cream
18. Wallpaper **Stipple** Apricot/Primrose
19. Wallpaper **Petite Fleur** Terracotta/Cream
20. Wallpaper **Wild Cherry** Sage/Cream
21. Tie-back **Smoke**
22. Fringing **Smoke**
23. Wallpaper Border F512 Kingfisher/Stone
24. Wallpaper Border F510 Smoke Multi Stone
25. Emulsion Paint **Stone**
26. Wallpaper Border T210 Smoke/Cream
27. Emulsion Paint **Light Sage**
28. Emulsion Paint **Light Kingfisher**
29. Emulsion Paint **Light Smoke**

DINING ROOM

One master print forms the basis for the decoration of this room, which has been carefully restored to what would probably have been its original early nineteenth century condition. The regularity of the stencil-like tulip print on the wallpaper and festoon blinds, provides the necessary formality for a dining room, without being too intense. Its tones of terracotta and green are totally in keeping with the warm earthy hues of ochre, Venetian red and green found in many Early American colour schemes, and form an effective and light-hearted combination with the stippled blue and stone background.

Wallpaper & Festoon Blinds in Country Furnishing Cotton:
Tulips, Multi Stone.

Armchair in Country Furnishing Cotton:
Simla, Multi Terracotta.

Cushion in Country Furnishing Cotton:
Pondicherry, Light Sage Multi White.

China:
Scottish Thistle, Burgundy/Sage/Cream.

19TH CENTURY HOUSE, SAG HARBOUR, NEW YORK

1. Wallpaper **Nutmeg** Sage/Cream
2. Braid **Sage**
3. Wallpaper **Wild Cherry** Sage/Cream
4. Braid **Kingfisher/Smoke**
5. Wallpaper **Infinity** Smoke/Cream
6. Plain Gimp **Terracotta**
7. Wallpaper **Wood Violet** Terracotta/Moss/Cream
8. Braid **Sage**
9. Wallpaper **Tulips** Multi Stone
10. Wallpaper Border F510 Smoke Multi Stone
11. Frilled Cushion **Cricket Stripe** Terracotta/Moss/Cream

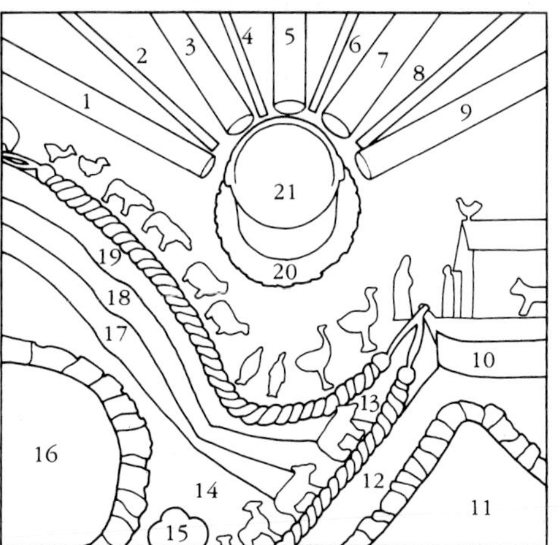

12. Country Furnishing Cotton **Cordelia** Multi Stone
13. Tie-back **Terracotta**
14. Country Furnishing Cotton **Wickerwork** Cream/Sage
15. Country Furnishing Cotton **Simla** Multi Terracotta
16. Frilled Cushion **Dandelion** Terracotta/Moss/Cream
17. Country Furnishing Cotton **Cricket Stripe** Terracotta/Moss/Cream
18. Country Furnishing Cotton **Nutmeg** Cream/Sage
19. Country Furnishing Cotton **Tulips** Multi Stone
20. Fringing **Terracotta**
21. Emulsion Paint **Stone**

BEDROOM, 19TH CENTURY HOUSE

Stripes make any room look smart and well planned, and in this case, very much in keeping with the house's nautical history. This small bedroom has all the ordered appearance of a nineteenth century sea-captain's cabin. The colour scheme is typical American Federal in different shades of cream, green and terracotta, whose slight variations in tone give it the natural look of having 'acquired' its furnishings rather than being deliberately contrived. Curtains, walls and bed are in a neat, three-colour stripe while an armchair is covered in a lively print of small diamonds and leaves on a bright terracotta ground. A touch of variety is added by the bolster on the bed, in an exotic, late eighteenth century print of flowers, berries and creepers.
These three totally different, yet complementary designs work together side by side to unify the room and give it a 'lived-in' appearance.

Main Photograph – Wallpaper:
Cricket Stripe, Terracotta/Moss/Cream.

Blind & Curtains in Country Furnishing Cotton:
Cricket Stripe, Terracotta/Moss/Cream.

Armchair in Country Furnishing Cotton:
Simla, Multi Terracotta.

Shown Below – Bed-cover in Country Furnishing Cotton:
Cricket Stripe, Terracotta/Moss/Cream.

Bolster in Chintz:
Hamilton, Terracotta Multi Cream.

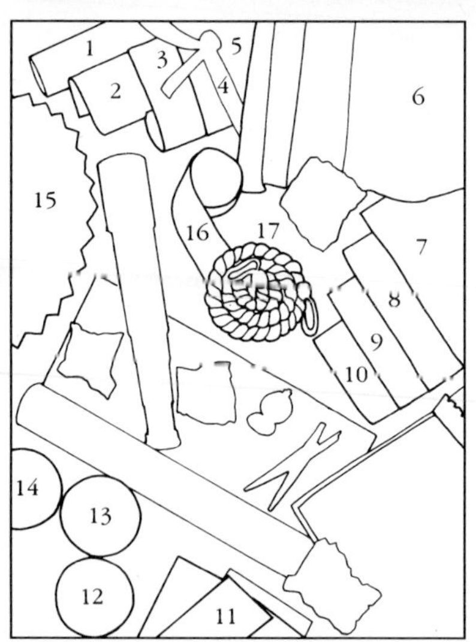

1. Wallpaper **Jocelyn** Terracotta Multi Cream
2. Wallpaper **Trellis** Terracotta/Cream
3. Wallpaper **Wood Violet** Terracotta/Moss/Cream
4. Plain Gimp **Terracotta**
5. Wallpaper **Cricket Stripe** Terracotta/Moss/Cream
6. Chintz **Hamilton** Terracotta Multi Cream
7. Country Furnishing Cotton **Dandelion** Terracotta/Moss/Green
8. Country Furnishing Cotton **Cricket Stripe** Terracotta/Moss/Cream
9. Country Furnishing Cotton **Delhi** Multi Salmon
10. Country Furnishing Cotton **Simla** Multi Terracotta
11. Ceramic Tiles **White** & Border Tiles **Terracotta**
12. Emulsion Paint **Pale Moss**
13. Gloss Paint **Terracotta**
14. Gloss Paint **Moss**
15. Pleated Lampshade **Terracotta**
16. Wallpaper Border F215 Terracotta/Tan/Cream
17. Tie-back **Terracotta**

MASTER BEDROOM, HOUSE IN SAG HARBOUR

NEW YORK

If any room in this house can be said to sum up the feeling of the American Federal style, then it is the master bedroom.

Here one finds late eighteenth century American decoration at its most basic, yet showing a strong individual character. The colours are blue and light stone – the traditional colours of the early American nation, used throughout the Federal period on everything from waistcoat linings to furniture cases. Here they have been put to more decorative uses, with considerable success. The curtains and elaborate bed-hangings are in a dot and square print originally used on popular tablecloths. This co-ordinates well with the similar border used on the bedcover and the simple symmetrical dot design discovered on the lining of a trunk, now used for the valance, armchair and the lining of the drapes. Cushions are covered in a traditional country gingham check, and a delicate botanical print, both in the same co-ordinating tones of blue and stone.

All of the designs have a rustic, hand-printed appearance, two basic colours being quite enough with which to create a complete decorative scheme firmly expressive of the tradition which fills this historic old house.

Walls:
White, Vinyl Matt Emulsion Paint.

Curtains in Country Furnishing Cotton:
Harbour, Kingfisher/Stone.

Bed-hanging in Country Furnishing Cotton:
Harbour, Kingfisher/Stone.

Bed-cover in Fabric Border on Plain Country Furnishing Cotton Base:
F512, Kingfisher/Stone & **Cream**.

Valance in Country Furnishing Cotton:
Sea Spray, Kingfisher/Stone.

Armchair in Country Furnishing Cotton:
Sea Spray, Kingfisher/Stone.

Cushion in Country Furnishing Cotton:
Edward, Kingfisher/Stone.

Cushion in Country Furnishing Cotton:
Gingham, Kingfisher Multi Cream.

PURE BRISTLES
TRADITIONAL
QUILTING

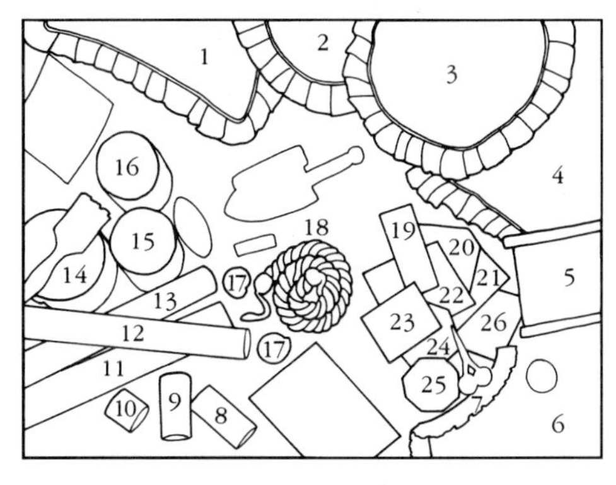

1. Frilled Cushion **Harbour** Kingfisher/Stone
2. Frilled Cushion **Paisley** Smoke/Kingfisher/Cream
3. Frilled Cushion **Sea Spray** Kingfisher/Stone
4. Frilled Cushion **Palmetto** Kingfisher/Burgundy/Cream
5. Braid **Kingfisher/Smoke**
6. Patchwork Quilt **Smoke**
7. Fringing **Smoke**
8. Wallpaper Border T210 Smoke/Cream
9. Wallpaper Border F512 Kingfisher/Stone
10. Wallpaper Border F510 Smoke Multi Stone
11. Wallpaper **Damask** Kingfisher/Smoke
12. Wallpaper **Edward** Kingfisher/Stone
13. Wallpaper **Infinity** Smoke/Cream
14. Emulsion Paint **Stone**
15. Emulsion Paint **Light Kingfisher**
16. Emulsion Paint **Light Smoke**
17. Plain Gimp **Smoke** & Braid **Smoke/Cream**
18. Tie-back **Smoke**
19. Country Furnishing Cotton **Harbour** Kingfisher/Stone
20. Country Furnishing Cotton **Paisley** Smoke/Kingfisher/Cream
21. Country Furnishing Cotton **Palmetto** Kingfisher/Burgundy/Cream
22. Country Furnishing Cotton **Damask** Kingfisher/Smoke
23. Country Furnishing Cotton **Gingham** Kingfisher Multi Cream
24. Country Furnishing Cotton **Edward** Kingfisher/Stone
25. Country Furnishing Cotton **Sea Spray** Kingfisher/Stone
26. Country Furnishing Cotton **Grapes** Smoke Multi Cream

WALLPAPER

The following 22 pages are intended as a helpful guide, by colourway, to the many possible combinations of co-ordinating designs in wallpaper and country furnishing cotton. On each page are shown swatches of the prints available in a certain colourway. Underneath each swatch are a number of symbols, explained in the key on this page, which show the range of products in which each particular print is available. A working example of how to use the pages is given below.
For a full price list please see the mail order insert in the back pages of this catalog.

Wallpaper: While paint produces a simple block effect, wallpaper, perhaps with a co-ordinating border, can provide vital interest at little expense.

This year sees the addition of fourteen new prints to give an even greater choice of colour co-ordination.

All Laura Ashley wallpaper is fully washable. Each roll measures 53cm (21in) in width and 10m (11yds) in length. The weight is carefully calculated at 135gsm. We recommend a light or medium weight cellulose-based wallpaper paste, and would also refer you at the time of hanging to the instructions on reverse of the wallpaper label. **$17.50** per roll.

Country Furnishing Cotton: produced in the tradition of the colourful cottons once found only in great houses, though since Victorian times more widely available, the 1985 collection is more versatile than ever before, offering a wide choice from traditional small floral prints, to larger, brighter and more formal designs. This 100% pure cotton fabric is available in 120cm (48in) widths. The maximum continuous length which can be supplied is 35m (38yds). It may be washed in warm or hot water (40°c) or dry cleaned and hot ironed. After the first wash it may shrink by between 3-5%. It should not be bleached. **$12.00** per yard.

COUNTRY FURNISHING COTTON

KINGFISHER
Damask
F526 Kingfisher/Smoke 326281
Sea Spray
F493 Kingfisher/Stone 323255
Harbour
F490 Kingfisher/Stone 324255
Edward
F456 Kingfisher/Stone 325255
Gingham
F386 Kingfisher Multi Cream 186498
Palmetto 184256
F303 Kingfisher/Burgundy/Cream
Antoinette
F354 Kingfisher/Stone 181255
Louis
F390 Kingfisher Multi Stone 182479
Kingfisher
020313

Shepherd's Purse
R193 Smoke/Cream 028013
Cordelia
F537 Multi Stone 328397
Paisley
F477 Smoke/Kingfisher/Cream 332500

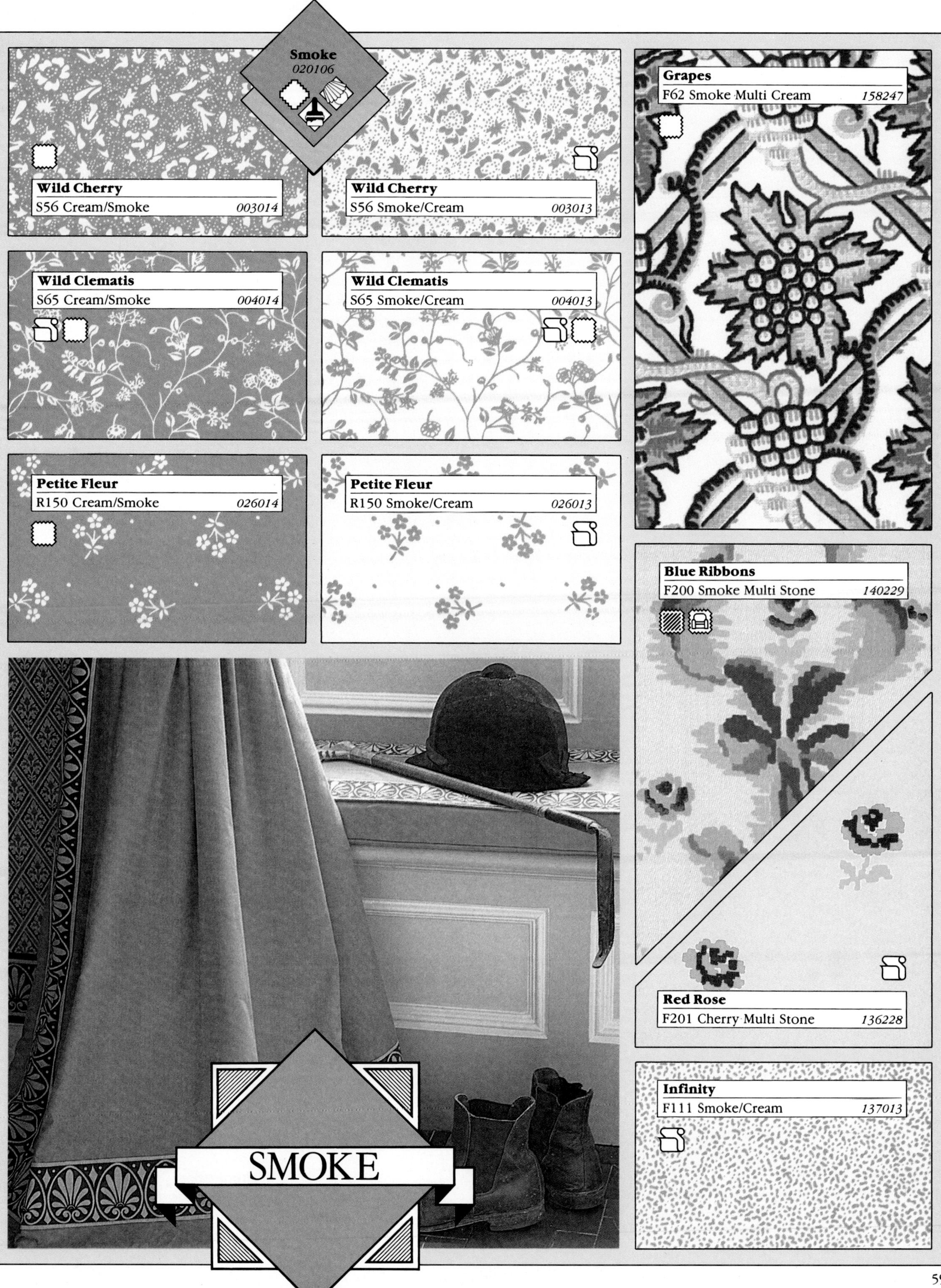
Smoke
020106
Wild Cherry
S56 Cream/Smoke 003014
Wild Cherry
S56 Smoke/Cream 003013
Wild Clematis
S65 Cream/Smoke 004014
Wild Clematis
S65 Smoke/Cream 004013
Petite Fleur
R150 Cream/Smoke 026014
Petite Fleur
R150 Smoke/Cream 026013
Grapes
F62 Smoke Multi Cream 158247
Blue Ribbons
F200 Smoke Multi Stone 140229
Red Rose
F201 Cherry Multi Stone 136228
Infinity
F111 Smoke/Cream 137013
SMOKE

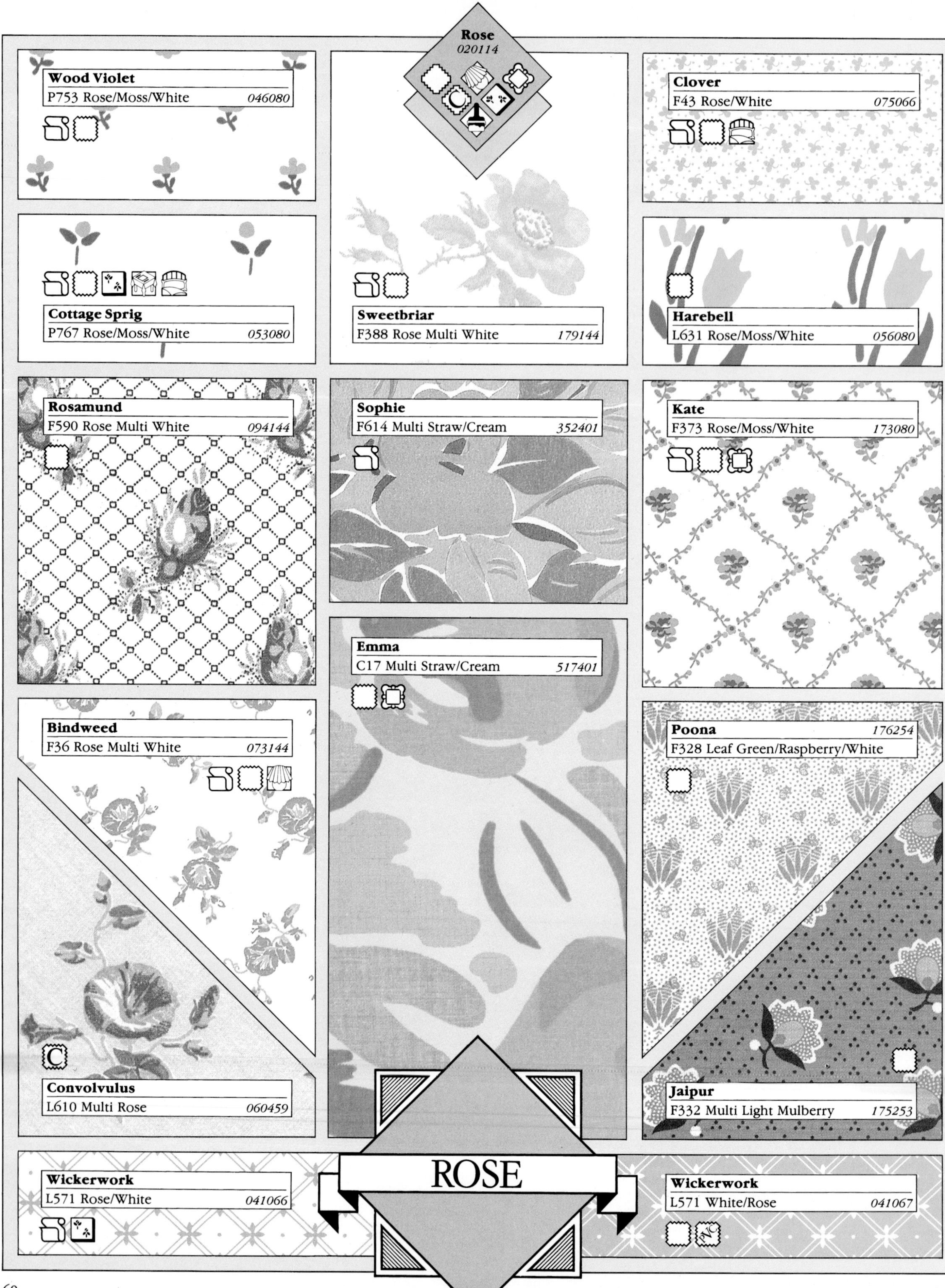
Rose
020114
Wood Violet
P753 Rose/Moss/White 046080
Clover
F43 Rose/White 075066
Cottage Sprig
P767 Rose/Moss/White 053080
Sweetbriar
F388 Rose Multi White 179144
Harebell
L631 Rose/Moss/White 056080
Rosamund
F590 Rose Multi White 094144
Sophie
F614 Multi Straw/Cream 352401
Kate
F373 Rose/Moss/White 173080
Emma
C17 Multi Straw/Cream 517401
Bindweed
F36 Rose Multi White 073144
Poona 176254
F328 Leaf Green/Raspberry/White
Convolvulus
L610 Multi Rose 060459
Jaipur
F332 Multi Light Mulberry 175253
Wickerwork
L571 Rose/White 041066
ROSE
Wickerwork
L571 White/Rose 041067

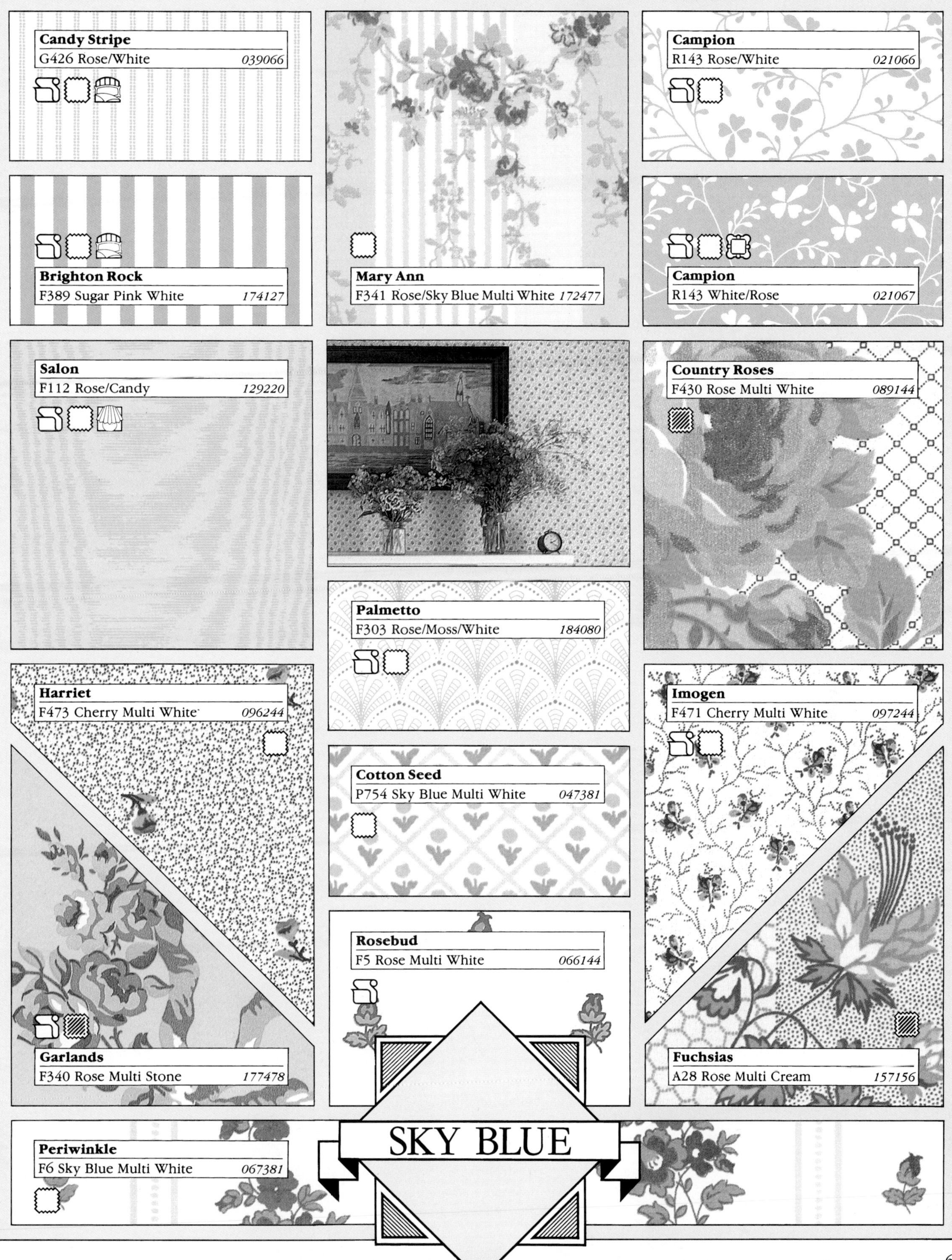
Candy Stripe
G426 Rose/White 039066
Brighton Rock
F389 Sugar Pink White 174127
Mary Ann
F341 Rose/Sky Blue Multi White 172477
Campion
R143 Rose/White 021066
Campion
R143 White/Rose 021067
Salon
F112 Rose/Candy 129220
Country Roses
F430 Rose Multi White 089144
Palmetto
F303 Rose/Moss/White 184080
Harriet
F473 Cherry Multi White 096244
Imogen
F471 Cherry Multi White 097244
Cotton Seed
P754 Sky Blue Multi White 047381
Rosebud
F5 Rose Multi White 066144
Garlands
F340 Rose Multi Stone 177478
Fuchsias
A28 Rose Multi Cream 157156
Periwinkle
F6 Sky Blue Multi White 067381
SKY BLUE

AQUAMARINE
Kew Gardens
F484 Mint Multi White 090396
Penelope
F535 Mint Multi White 095396
020340
Aquamarine
Palmetto 184267
F303 Apricot/Aqua./Apricot Wash
Salon
F112 Mint/Aquamarine 129212
Regency Stripe
F374 Aquamarine/Apricot/White 197268

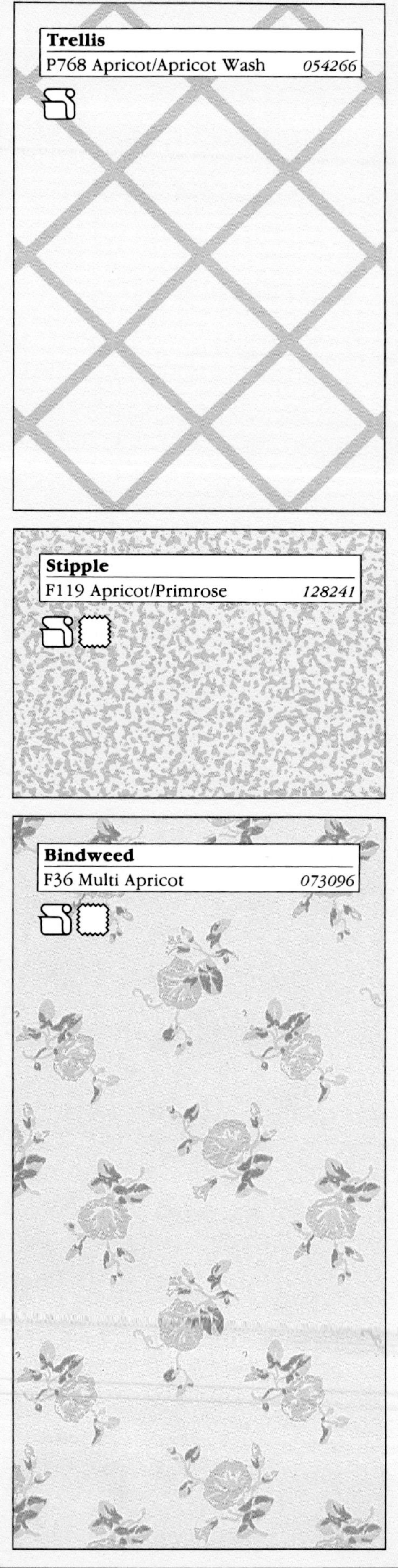
Trellis
P768 Apricot/Apricot Wash 054266
Stipple
F119 Apricot/Primrose 128241
Bindweed
F36 Multi Apricot 073096

APRICOT
Apricot
020116
Floribunda
L577 Multi Apricot 042096
Clarissa
F45 Apricot Multi White 076146
Palmetto
F303 Aquamarine/Apricot/White 184268
Salon
F112 Apricot/Apricot Wash 129266
Regency Stripe
F374 Apricot/Aquamarine/White 197265

PLUM
Wild Clematis
S65 Plum/Cream 004011
Wild Clematis
S65 Cream/Plum 004012
Nutmeg
S49 Plum/Cream 015011
Clifton Castle
F353 Cream/Plum 183012
Nutmeg
S49 Cream/Plum 015012
Paisley
F477 Plum/Saddle/Cream 332264
Plum
020112
Wild Cherry
S56 Cream/Plum 003012

Dandelion
F335 Plum/Sage/Cream 302447
Michaelmas
P769 Plum/Sand/Cream 055223
Malcolm
F403 Multi Cream 088395
Cricket Stripe
F369 Plum/Saddle/Cream 185264
Trellis
P768 Sand/Cream 054210
SADDLE
Nutmeg
S49 Saddle/Sand 015002
Rawalpindi
F330 Multi Cinnamon 225271

Palmetto
F303 Sage/Cherry/White 184273
Nutmeg
S49 Sage/Cream 015032
Nutmeg
S49 Cream/Sage 015033
Light Sage
020350
Indienne
F538 Multi All-Spice 333399
Pondicherry
F339 Light Sage Multi White 304484
SAGE
Simla
F516 Multi All-Spice 331399
Wild Cherry
S56 Sage/Cream 003032
Wickerwork
L571 Sage/Cream 041032
Wickerwork
L571 Cream/Sage 041033

White Bower
F364 Dark Green Multi Cream 195482
C
Palmetto 184263
F303 Dark Green/Raspberry/Sand
Florentina
F358 Dark Green Multi Stone 192496
Damask
F526 Dark Green/Mid Green 326499
DARK GREEN
Favorita
F206 Dark Green Multi Sand 144230
Jessica 143387
F207 Dk.Green/Raspberry Multi Sand

Nutmeg
S49 Burgundy/White 015086
Florentina
F358 Burgundy Multi Stone 192481
Michaelmas
P769 Burgundy/Sand/White 055185
Scottish Thistle
F4 Burgundy/Sage/Cream 065188
Trellis
P768 Sand/White 054038
Nutmeg
S49 White/Burgundy 015084
Paisley Stripe
F351 Burgundy/Navy/Stone 188259
Wild Damson
F344 Burgundy/Cream 193208
Blazer Stripe
F384 Coriander/Burgundy 230128
Basketweave
F500 Burgundy/Cream 341208
BURGUNDY
Tapestry
F64 Multi Burgundy 156243
Venetia
F99 Burgundy/Gold 146232

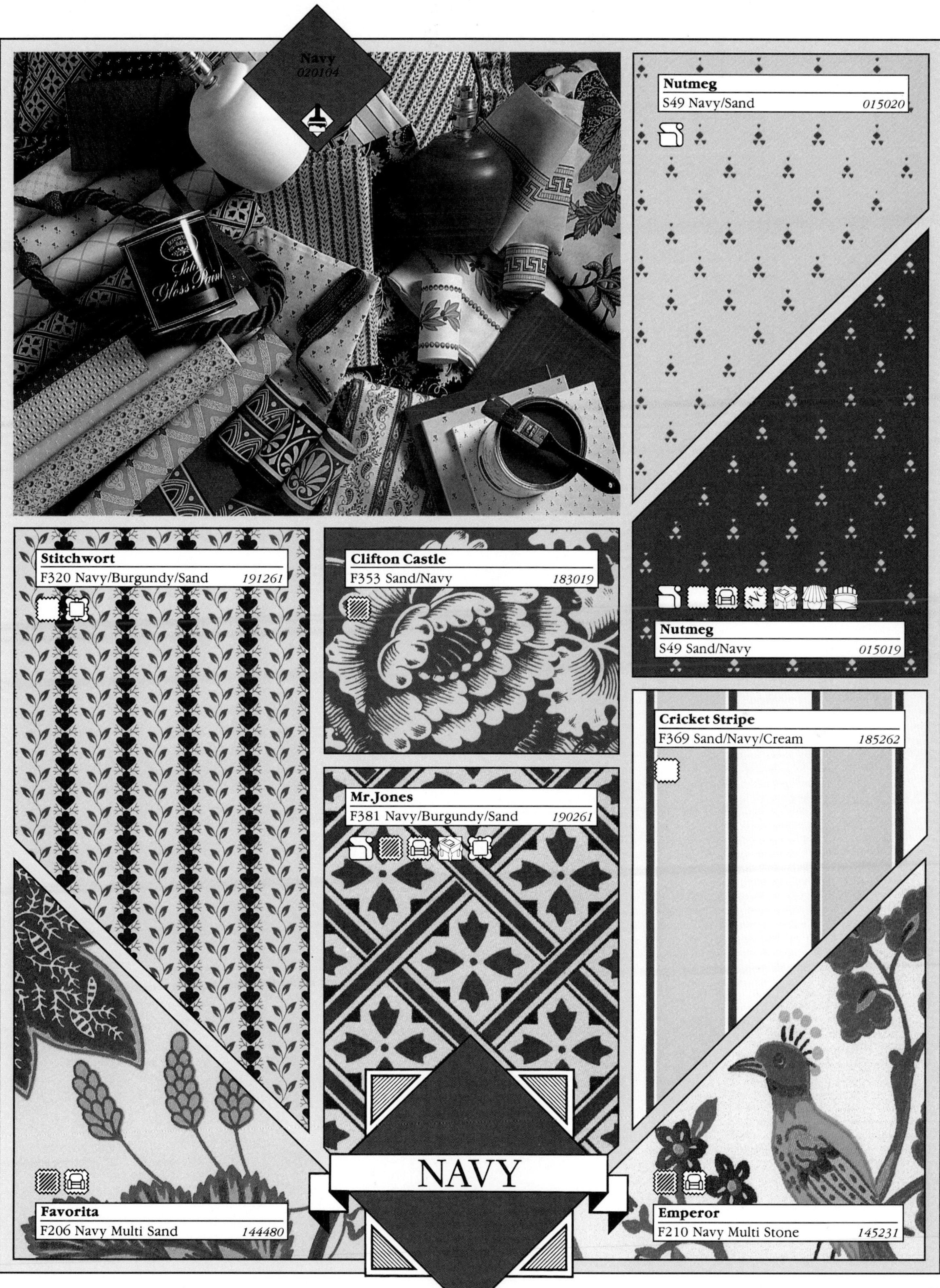
Navy
020104
Satin Gloss Paint
Nutmeg
S49 Navy/Sand 015020
Stitchwort
F320 Navy/Burgundy/Sand 191261
Clifton Castle
F353 Sand/Navy 183019
Nutmeg
S49 Sand/Navy 015019
Cricket Stripe
F369 Sand/Navy/Cream 185262
Mr.Jones
F381 Navy/Burgundy/Sand 190261
NAVY
Favorita
F206 Navy Multi Sand 144480
Emperor
F210 Navy Multi Stone 145231

SAND
Parapet
F378 Taupe/White 180130
Joy
F125 Sand Multi White 141139
English Garden
F367 Taupe Multi White 178486
Albert
F288 Oak Multi Sand 339502
Wickerwork
L571 Sand/White 041038
Wickerwork
L571 White/Sand 041068
Shepherd's Purse
R193 Sand/White 028038
Salon
F112 Sand/White 129038

Emmeline
F127 Sand Multi White 147139

Sand
020109
Gothic Trellis
F352 Multi Sand 194234
Rectory Garden
F316 Raspberry/Moss/Stone 199272
Deauville
F559 Oak Multi Stone 337509
Trellis
P768 Sand/White 054038
Nutmeg
S49 White/Sand 015068
Trellis
P768 Sand/Cream 054210

Clifton Castle
F353 Cream/Sand 183129

Dandelion
F335 Terracotta/Moss/Cream 302270
Tulips
F488 Multi Stone 327397
Shepherd's Purse
R193 Terracotta/Cream 028029
Emperor
F210 Terracotta Multi Cream 145233
Wild Cherry
S56 Terracotta/Cream 003029
Marble
F628 Greengage Multi Stone 299505
Milfoil
L570 Cream/Terracotta 040030
Hamilton
F505 Terracotta Multi Cream 092233
C
Queen Anne's Needlework
F10 Terracotta/Oak/Cream 070452
TERRACOTTA
Jocelyn 342233
F544 Terracotta
Multi Cream

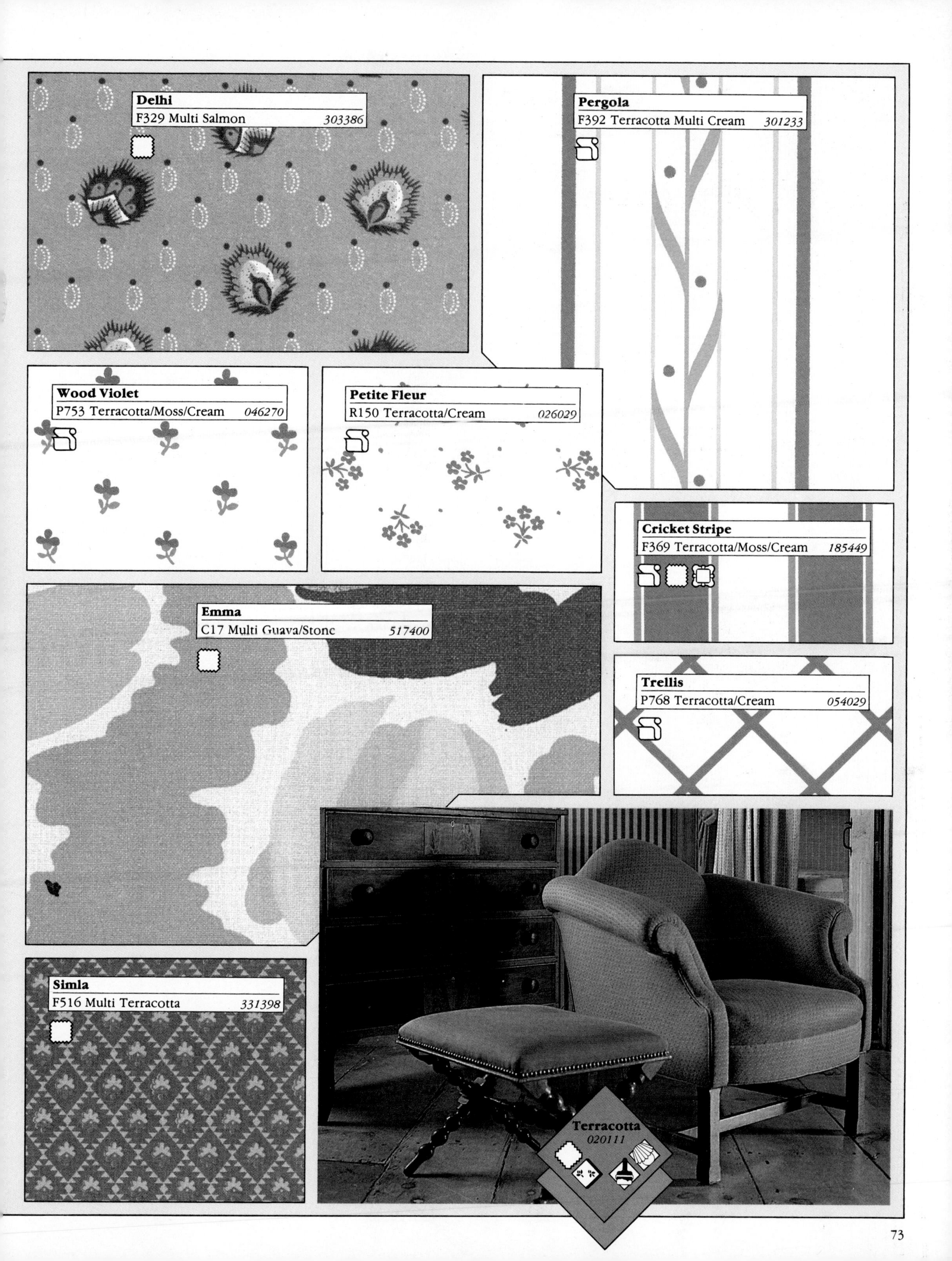

Delhi
F329 Multi Salmon 303386
Pergola
F392 Terracotta Multi Cream 301233
Wood Violet
P753 Terracotta/Moss/Cream 046270
Petite Fleur
R150 Terracotta/Cream 026029
Cricket Stripe
F369 Terracotta/Moss/Cream 185449
Emma
C17 Multi Guava/Stone 517400
Trellis
P768 Terracotta/Cream 054029
Simla
F516 Multi Terracotta 331398
Terracotta
020111

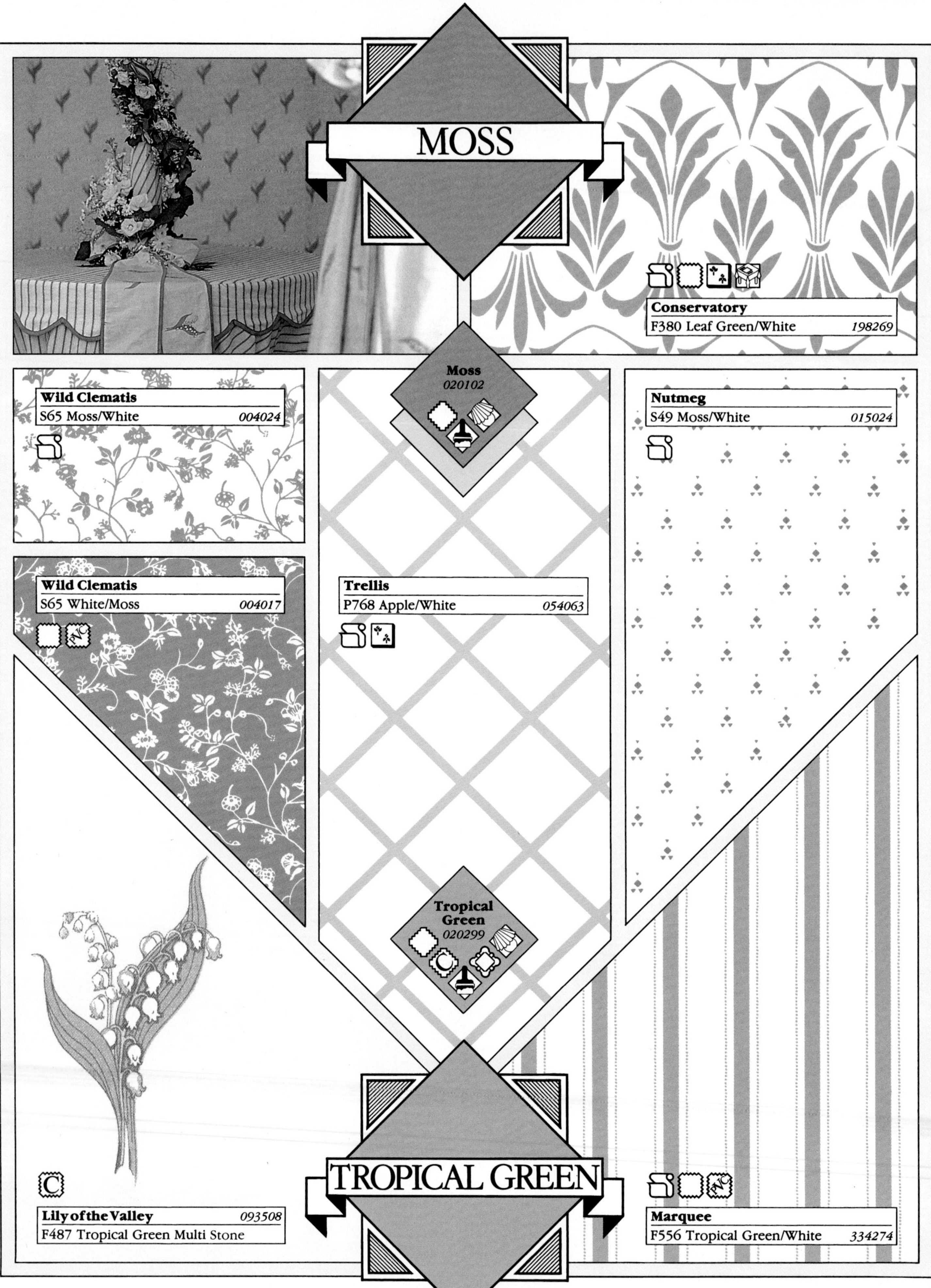
MOSS
Conservatory
F380 Leaf Green/White 198269
Wild Clematis
S65 Moss/White 004024
Moss
020102
Nutmeg
S49 Moss/White 015024
Wild Clematis
S65 White/Moss 004017
PVC
Trellis
P768 Apple/White 054063
Tropical
Green
020299
C
Lily of the Valley 093508
F487 Tropical Green Multi Stone
TROPICAL GREEN
PVC
Marquee
F556 Tropical Green/White 334274

CHINA BLUE
Floribunda
L577 Multi China Blue 042093
China Blue
020105
Nutmeg
S49 White/China Blue 015091
Cottage Sprig
P767 China Blue/Apple/White 053171
Ming
F132 China Blue/Sapphire/White 135162
DENIM
Henley
F568 Denim Multi White 335506
Dandelion 302448
F335 Denim/Tropical Green/White

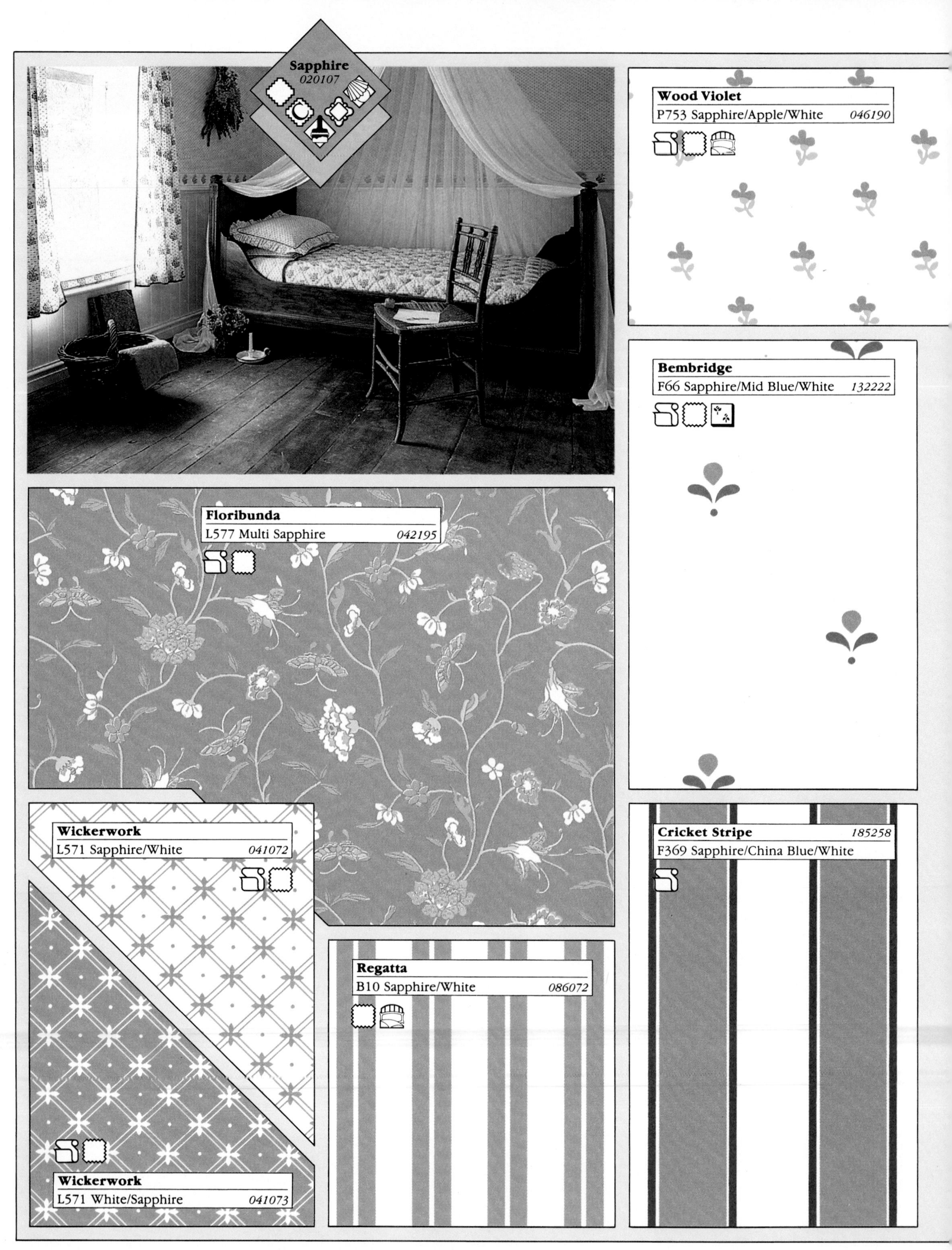
Sapphire
020107
Wood Violet
P753 Sapphire/Apple/White 046190
Bembridge
F66 Sapphire/Mid Blue/White 132222
Floribunda
L577 Multi Sapphire 042195
Wickerwork
L571 Sapphire/White 041072
Cricket Stripe 185258
F369 Sapphire/China Blue/White
Regatta
B10 Sapphire/White 086072
Wickerwork
L571 White/Sapphire 041073

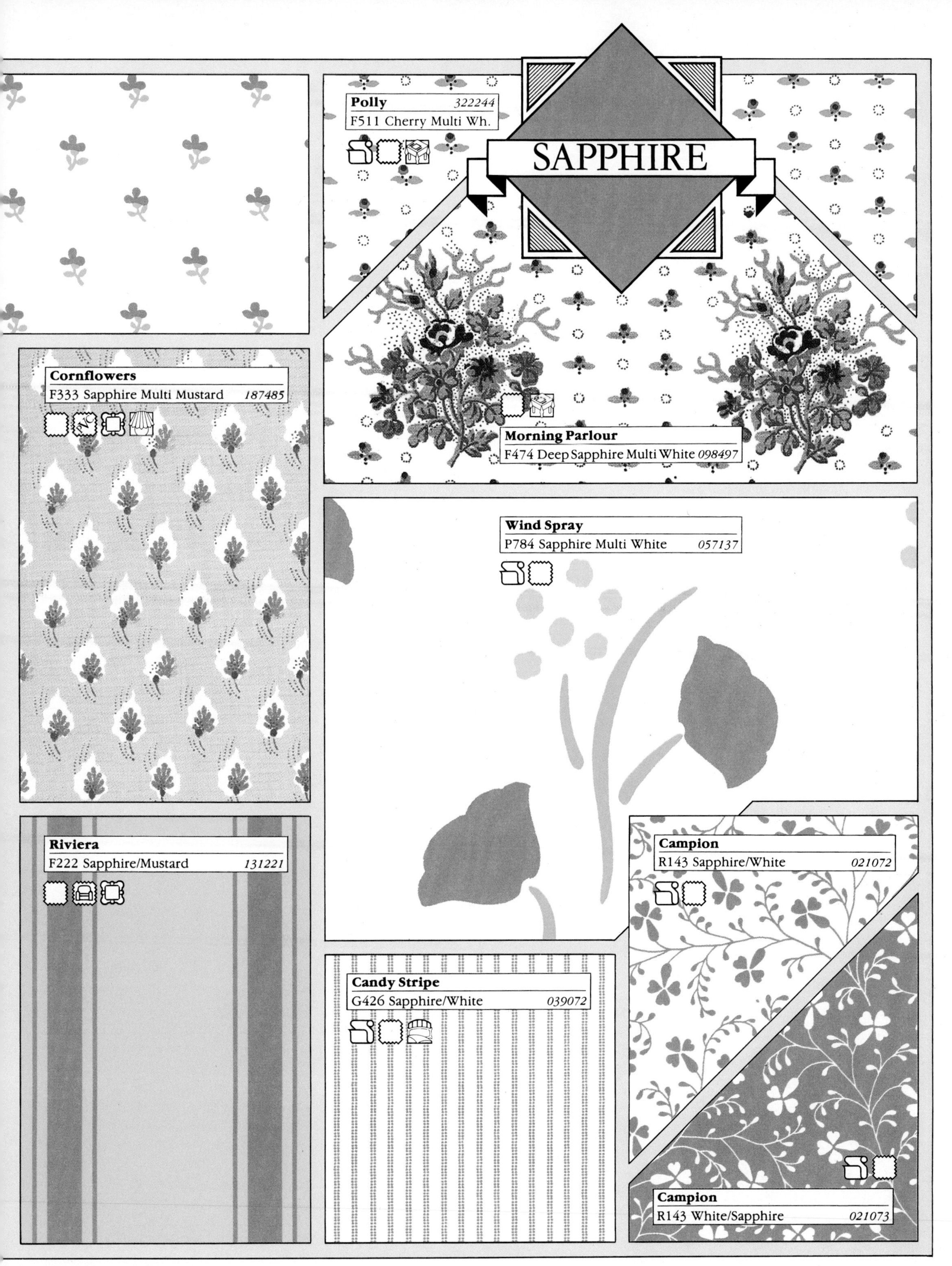
SAPPHIRE
Polly 322244
F511 Cherry Multi Wh.
Cornflowers
F333 Sapphire Multi Mustard 187485
Morning Parlour
F474 Deep Sapphire Multi White 098497
Wind Spray
P784 Sapphire Multi White 057137
Riviera
F222 Sapphire/Mustard 131221
Campion
R143 Sapphire/White 021072
Candy Stripe
G426 Sapphire/White 039072
Campion
R143 White/Sapphire 021073

MUSTARD
Trellis
P768 Mustard/White 054005
Trefoil
P752 White/Mustard 045001
Midsummer
F40 Mustard Multi White 074148
Meadow Flowers
F42 Poppy Multi White 078143
Floribunda
L577 Multi White 042242

POPPY
Wood Violet
P753 Mustard/Apple/White 046194
Gingham
F386 Poppy Multi White 186143
Summertime
F557 Multi Poppy 336094
Poppy
020113
Floribunda
L577 Multi Poppy 042094
Cottage Sprig
P767 Poppy/Apple/White 053169

Laura Ashley drawing room fabric is a cotton sateen cloth, heavier than country furnishing cotton, and particularly suitable for curtains and light upholstery. Cotton sateen was introduced in the late Victorian era and this up-to-date equivalent retains a sophisticated finish, lending itself to the larger, more formal prints in the collection, including three important new designs for 1985.

The fabric is printed in 120cm (45in) widths using high-quality, light-resistant dyes, and can be washed in warm water to 40°c and medium-hot ironed, or dry cleaned. It should not be bleached. The maximum continuous length which can be supplied is 35 yards. Please note that swatches are shown at 25% of their actual size.

$16.50 per yard

Kew Gardens F484 Mint Multi White *090396*

Emmeline F127 Sand Multi White *147139*

Garlands F340 Rose Multi Stone *177478*

Malcolm F403 Multi Cream *088395*

Clifton Castle F353 Cream/Plum *183012*

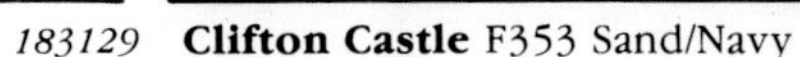

Clifton Castle F353 Cream/Sand *183129*

Clifton Castle F353 Sand/Navy *183019*

Favorita F206 Dark Green Multi Sand *144230*

Favorita F206 Navy Multi Sand *144480*

Venetia F99 Burgundy/Gold *146232*

Michaelmas P769 Plum/Sand/Cream *055223*

Michaelmas P769 Burgundy/Sand/White *055185*

Mr.Jones F381 Navy/Burgundy/Sand *190261*

Country Roses F430 Rose Multi White *089144*

Antoinette F354 Kingfisher/Stone *181255*

Louis F390 Kingfisher Multi Stone *182479*

Jessica F207 Dk Green/Raspberry Multi Sand *143387*

Fuchsias A28 Rose Multi Cream *157156*

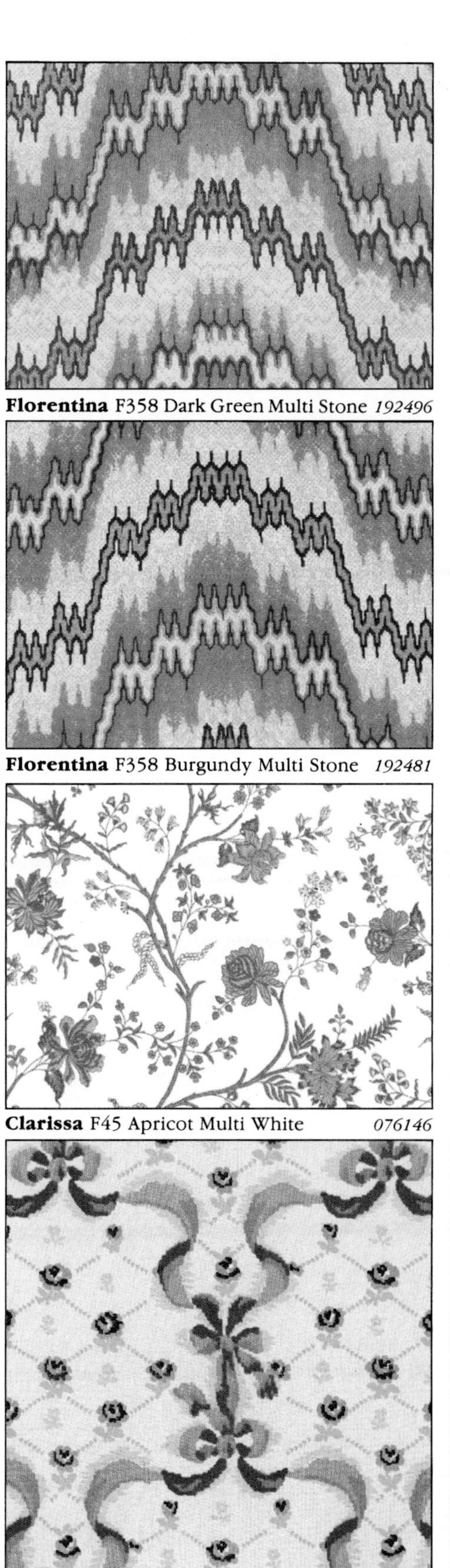

Florentina F358 Dark Green Multi Stone *192496*

Florentina F358 Burgundy Multi Stone *192481*

Clarissa F45 Apricot Multi White *076146*

Blue Ribbons F200 Smoke Multi Stone *140229*

Emperor F210 Terracotta Multi Cream *145233*

Emperor F210 Navy Multi Stone *145231*

Tapestry F64 Multi Burgundy *156243*

CHINTZ

The word chintz is derived from the Hindi word 'chitta' meaning spotted cloth, the original chintz being made in India for export to Europe where it has been popular since the seventeenth century.

Laura Ashley chintz is produced in a number of traditional designs with a full glaze finish making it as attractive as its eighteenth century predecessor, adding a brilliant lustre to all curtains, drapes, pelmets, blinds and decorative chair covers. This year, two new prints and six striking plain colours are added to the growing collection.

This 100% pure cotton fabric is available in 120cm (48in) widths. The maximum continuous length which can be supplied is 35 yards. To retain the full glaze, chintz should be dry cleaned only.

Please note that swatches are shown at 25% of their actual size.

$15.50 per yard

English Garden F367 Taupe Multi White *178486*

White Bower F364 Dk Green Multi Cream *195482*

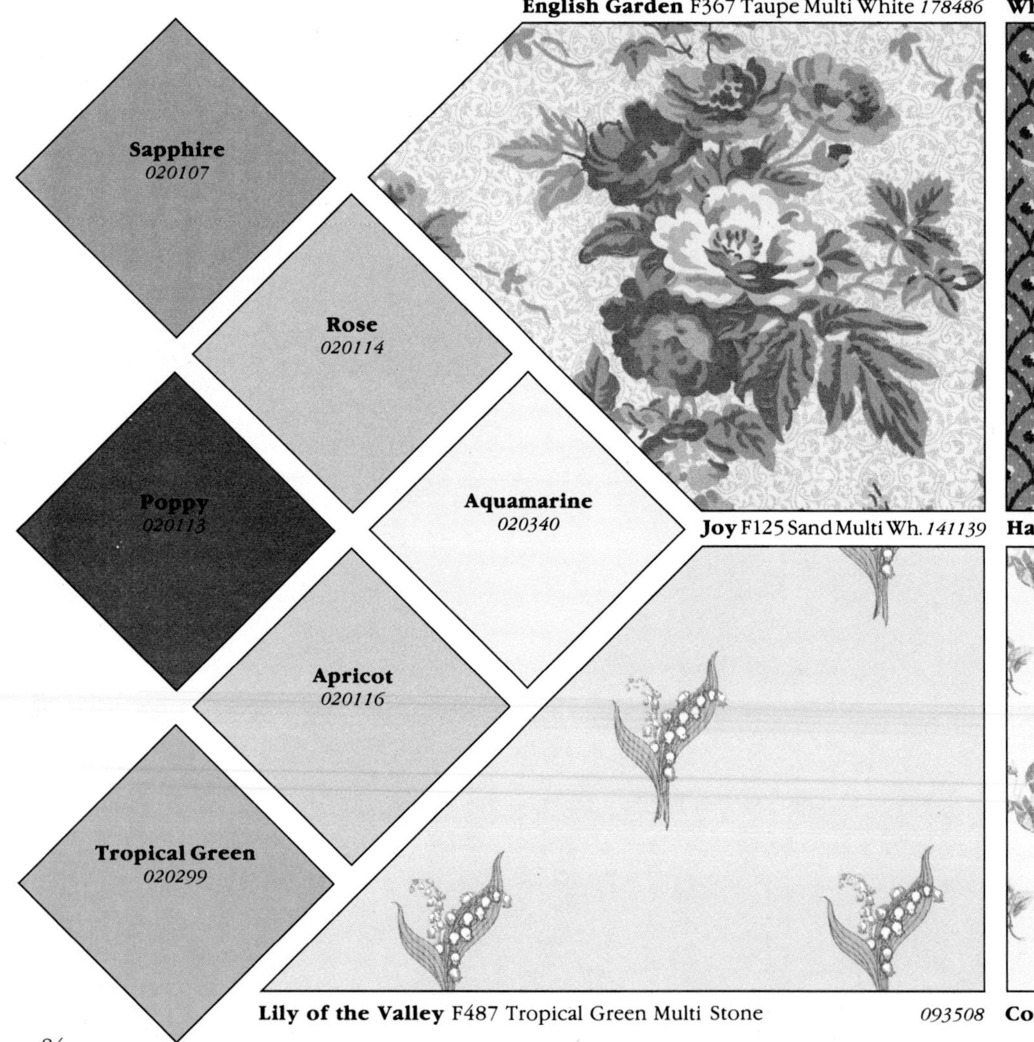

Joy F125 Sand Multi Wh. *141139*

Hamilton F505 Terracotta Multi Cream *092233*

Lily of the Valley F487 Tropical Green Multi Stone *093508*

Convolvulus L610 Multi Rose *060459*

UPHOLSTERY FABRIC

Although it may not necessarily have to contend with the heavy wear and tear of children and dogs, a hard-wearing upholstery fabric is essential in most households. With this in mind, a sturdy cotton, suitable for both light upholstery and loose covers, has been developed in a selection of popular prints, including this year, six new introductions. This specially woven heavy-weight fabric is designed to be attractive as well as durable, and while being particularly suitable for loose covers and upholstery, may also be used successfully for curtains, cushions and blinds.

It is available in 150cm (59in) widths and should be washed in warm to medium water (40°c), and a medium to hot iron should be used. It is suitable for dry cleaning but should not be bleached. The maximum continuous length which can be supplied is 25 yards.

$23.50 per yard

Paisley F477 Smoke/Kingfisher/Cream *332500*

Paisley F477 Plum/Saddle/Cream *332264*

Palmetto F303 Dk.Green/Raspberry/Sand *184263*

Riviera F222 Sapphire/Mustard *131221*

Emperor F210 Terracotta Multi Cream *145233*

Favorita F206 Dark Green Multi Sand *144230*

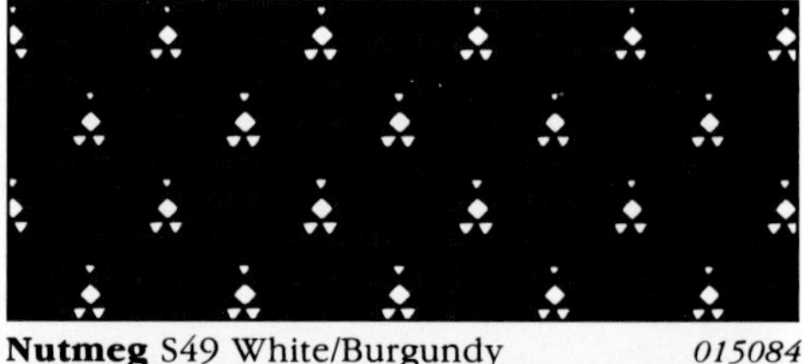

Nutmeg S49 White/Burgundy *015084*

Emperor F210 Navy Multi Stone *145231*

Favorita F206 Navy Multi Sand *144480*

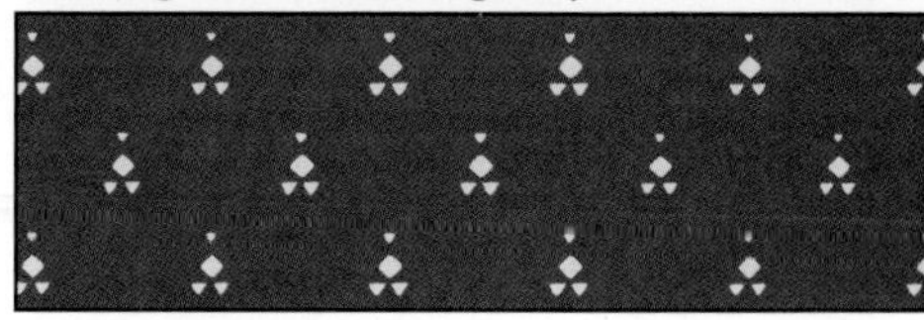

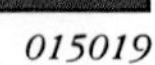

Nutmeg S49 Sand/Navy *015019*

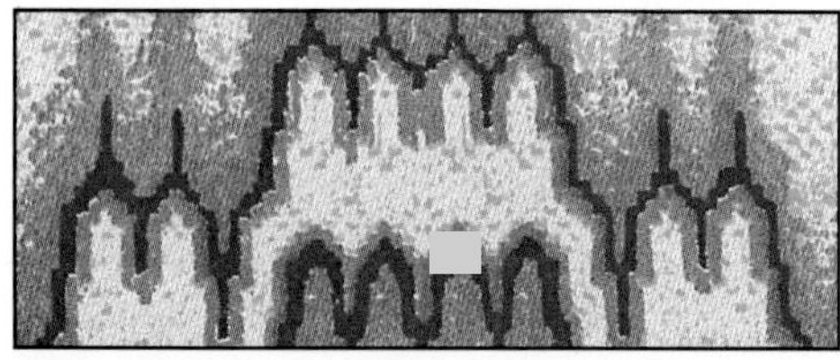

Florentina F358 Dark Green Multi Stone *192496*

Mr Jones F381 Navy/Burgundy/Sand *190261*

Blue Ribbons F200 Smoke Multi Stone *140229*

PLASTIC COATED FABRIC

Wild Clematis S65 White/Moss *004017*

Dandelion F335 Terracotta/Moss/Cream *302270*

Wickerwork L571 White/Rose *041067*

Cornflowers F333 Sapphire Multi Mustard *187485*

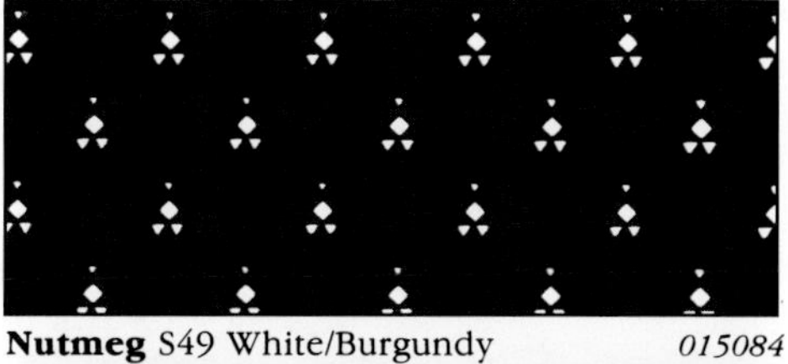

Nutmeg S49 White/Burgundy *015084*

Nutmeg S49 Sand/Navy *015019*

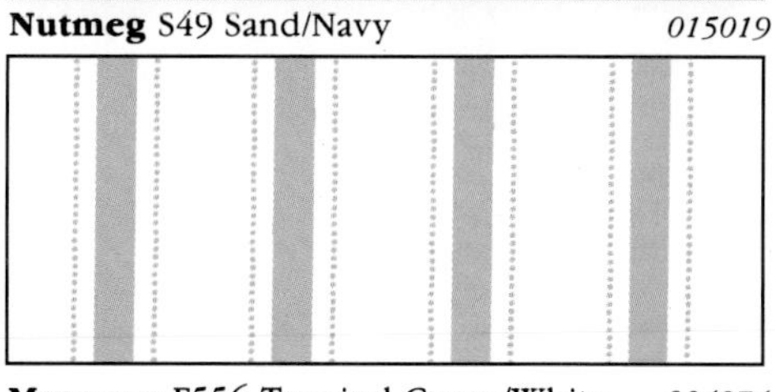

Marquee F556 Tropical Green/White *334274*

In the tradition of Victorian oil cloth, Laura Ashley presents a new cotton fabric with a double thickness impermeable P.V.C. coating. This heavy plasticised country furnishing cotton, in a number of attractive prints can be used, just as its Victorian counterpart, in kitchens, nurseries and bathrooms. In fact anywhere around the house where an easily cleaned fabric may be needed. The fabric may be cut, sewn and hemmed, and is available in designs specially chosen to co-ordinate well with any existing colour scheme.

The fabric, which is approximately 115cms (45ins) wide should not be washed or dry cleaned, but simply wiped with a damp cloth. Since it is coated on one side only it is not suitable for shower curtains, (see page 115 for the new Laura Ashley shower curtain kit). The maximum continuous length which can be supplied is 25yards.

$17.00 per yard

WALLPAPER & FABRIC BORDERS

Borders are an instant and inexpensive way of adding a touch of character to any empty room. On plain walls at dado or cornice level, wallpaper borders limit large expanses of paint, while used with a co-ordinating wallpaper, they pick out particular colours and give the design greater clarity and impact. They can also be used effectively to add depth to a staircase wall, or to outline a window, door or fireplace, so defining the space of any room.

Fabric borders can be equally as effective. Used on curtains, pelmets, cushions, tablecloths, bedcovers, tie-backs or blinds they make an attractive alternative to braid or fringe. In fourteen designs and various colourways in country furnishing cotton, with a selvedge of 4cm (1 ½ in) for hemming, these borders may be ordered by the yard.

Laura Ashley wallpaper borders are available in eighteen designs, in a number of colourways. This year, eight new prints have been introduced to make co-ordination with the rest of the collection even easier.

Wallpaper borders have the same washable surface as Laura Ashley wallpaper, and are sold in 10m (11 yd) lengths, either separately (110mm/4 ¼ in wide) or, depending on design, in packs of two (55mm/2 ¼ in wide).

Please note that all swatches are shown half actual size.

Wallpaper Borders (per pack)	**$6.50**
Fabric Borders, 110mm/4 ¼ in wide (per yard)	**$4.50**
Fabric Borders, 55mm/2 ¼ in wide (per yard)	**$3.50**

Wallpaper Borders **Fabric Borders**

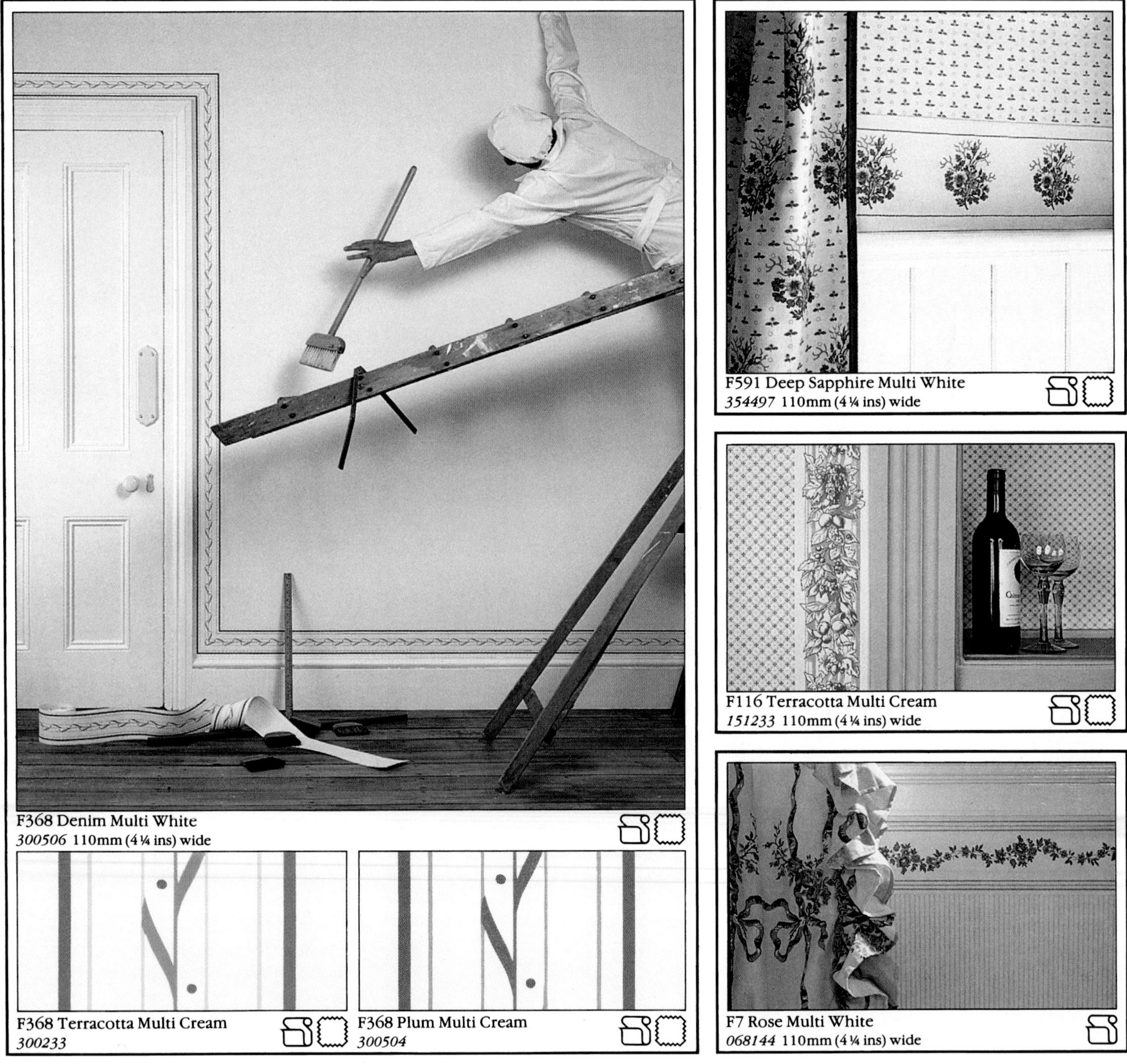

F368 Denim Multi White
300506 110mm (4 ¼ ins) wide

F368 Terracotta Multi Cream
300233

F368 Plum Multi Cream
300504

F591 Deep Sapphire Multi White
354497 110mm (4 ¼ ins) wide

F116 Terracotta Multi Cream
151233 110mm (4 ¼ ins) wide

F7 Rose Multi White
068144 110mm (4 ¼ ins) wide

F510 Rose Multi White
350144 55mm (2 ¼ ins) wide

F510 Tan Multi Sand
350507

F510 Smoke Multi Stone
350229

F512 Kingfisher/Stone
346255 55mm (2 ¼ ins) wide

F594 Black/White
356027 55mm (2 ¼ ins) wide

L631 Sapphire/Apple/White
056190

L631 Rose/Moss/White
056080

L631 Poppy/Apple/White
056169

L631 China Blue/Apple/White
056171 55mm (2 ¼ ins) wide

F215 Terracotta/Tan/Cream
150487 55mm (2 ¼ ins) wide

F215 Navy/Tan/Sand
150456

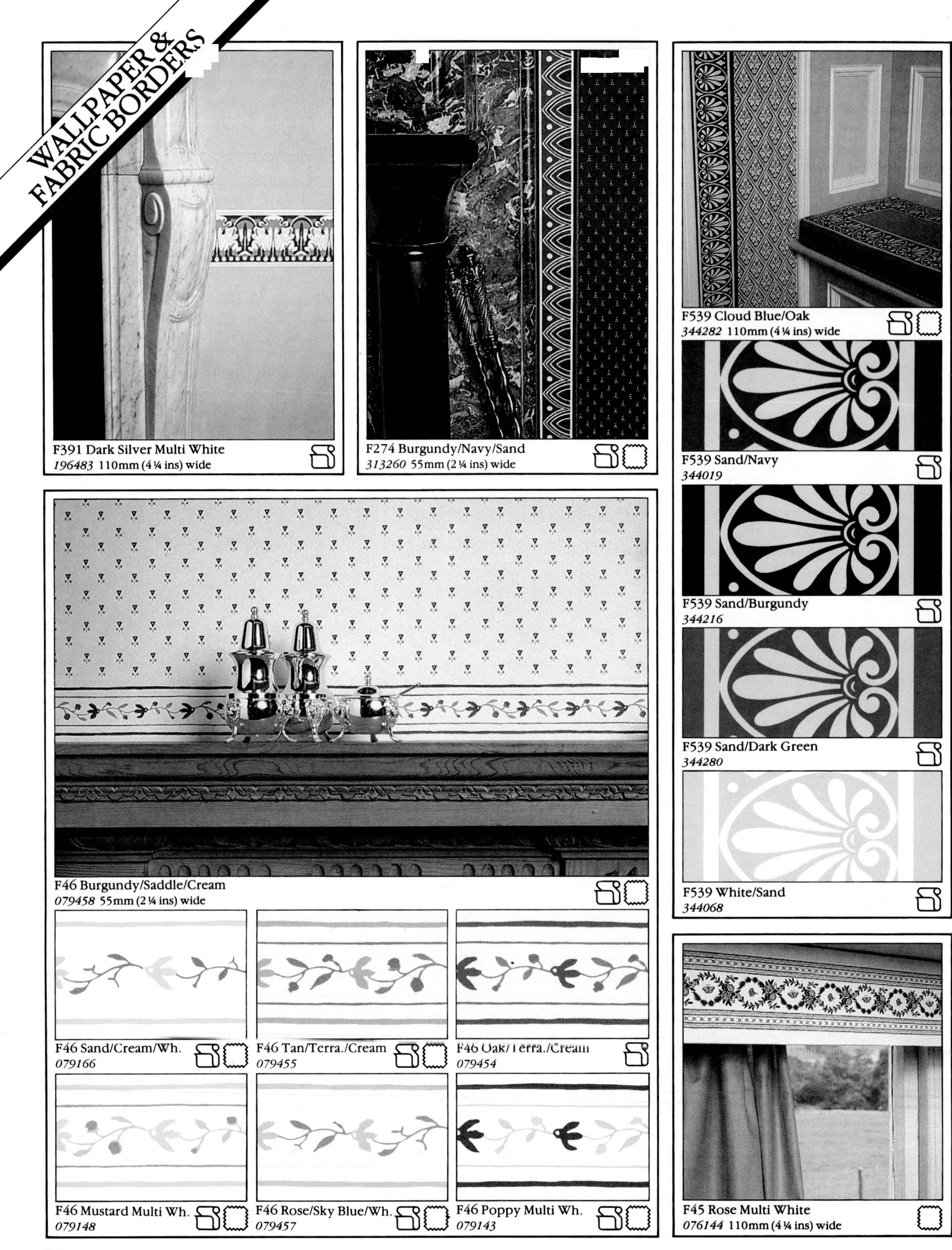

WALLPAPER & FABRIC BORDERS

F391 Dark Silver Multi White
196483 110mm (4¼ ins) wide

F274 Burgundy/Navy/Sand
313260 55mm (2¼ ins) wide

F539 Cloud Blue/Oak
344282 110mm (4¼ ins) wide

F539 Sand/Navy
344019

F539 Sand/Burgundy
344216

F539 Sand/Dark Green
344280

F539 White/Sand
344068

F46 Burgundy/Saddle/Cream
079458 55mm (2¼ ins) wide

F46 Sand/Cream/Wh.
079166

F46 Tan/Terra./Cream
079455

F46 Oak/Terra./Cream
079454

F46 Mustard Multi Wh.
079148

F46 Rose/Sky Blue/Wh.
079457

F46 Poppy Multi Wh.
079143

F45 Rose Multi White
076144 110mm (4¼ ins) wide

P897 Apricot/Moss/White
063175 110mm (4¼ ins) wide

P897 Rose/Moss/White
063080

P897 Sapphire/Moss/White
063088

F627 Rose Multi White
355144 110mm (4¼ ins) wide

F551 Multi Oak
349403 55mm (2¼ ins) wide

T210 Sapphire/White
029072 55mm (2¼ ins) wide

T210 Smoke/Cream
029013

T210 Plum/Cream
029011

F221 Navy Multi Sand
152480 110mm (4¼ ins) wide

F221 Burgundy Multi Cream
152238

T210 Rose/White
029066

T210 White/Burgundy
029084

T210 Moss/White
029024

To add the finishing touches to your interior, Laura Ashley presents an exciting new selection of decorative trimmings:

Plain Gimp
In 100% viscose, 1.5cm (⅝in) wide gimp is offered in eleven colourways to co-ordinate with the rest of the home decoration collection. Sold by the yard, it provides the perfect border to define lines of upholstery, cushions and lampshades.
$2.00 per yard

Fringing
In 100% viscose, fringing can be used to great effect to enhance curtains, cushions and lampshades. In eleven co-ordinating colourways it is available by the yard in 3.5 cm (1⅜in) widths.
$4.00 per yard

Tie-backs
An attractive finishing touch for any curtains or drapes. Made in eleven colourways from twisted cord, each tie-back is 100cm (39½in) long and 2.25cm (⅞in) wide, finished with pommel ends and simple loop fittings. 55% cotton, 45% viscose.
$14.00 per pair

Folded Bias Binding

This co-ordinating binding is ideal as a neat piping for cushions, loose covers, and unfinished edges. Cut on the bias and folded, this 100% cotton binding is 2.5 cm (1 in) wide. Not available in the U.S.A.

Colour	Code	Colour	Code
White	*020100*	**Cream**	*020110*
Aquamarine	*020340*	**Sand**	*020109*
Rose	*020114*	**Sky Blue**	*020341*
Sapphire	*020107*	**Apricot**	*020116*
Plum	*020112*	**Smoke**	*020106*
Tan	*020122*	**Moss**	*020102*
Apple	*020103*	**Mustard**	*020118*
Poppy	*020113*	**China Blue**	*020105*
Sage	*020123*	**Saddle**	*020120*
Terracotta	*020111*	**Dark Green**	*020101*
Navy	*020104*	**Burgundy**	*020115*

Braid

Add a touch of flamboyance to all upholstery, cushions and lampshades with this smart, two-tone braid sold by the yard in eight co-ordinated colourways. 1.5 cm (⅝ in) wide. 80% viscose, 20% cotton. Not available in the U.S.A.

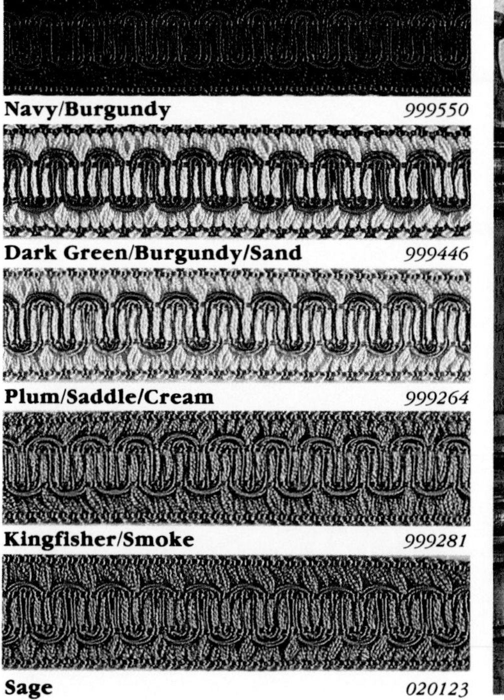

Navy/Burgundy *999550*

Dark Green/Burgundy/Sand *999446*

Plum/Saddle/Cream *999264*

Kingfisher/Smoke *999281*

Sage *020123*

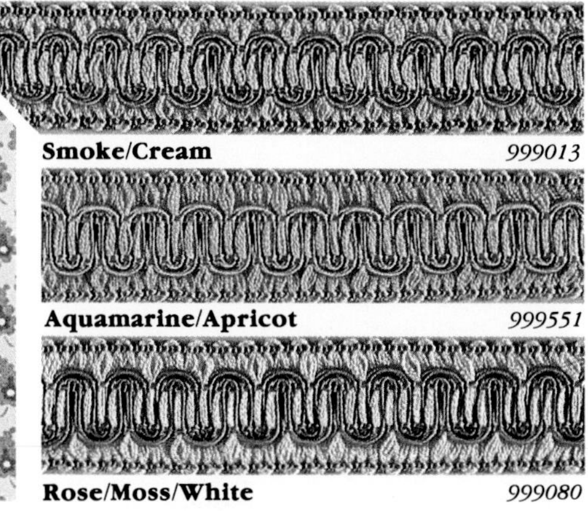

Smoke/Cream *999013*

Aquamarine/Apricot *999551*

Rose/Moss/White *999080*

VINYL FLAT EMULSION PAINT

A few coats of paint, perhaps with a decorative printed border, can transform a room quickly and easily at very little expense. A quantity of water or white added to emulsion will produce a softer tone of the same hue, while many interesting effects can be obtained by such techniques as dragging, washing and stippling.
A wide range of colours, from warm reds and pinks to cool blues and greens, have been specially formulated to co-ordinate with Laura Ashley fabrics, producing a variety of totally different atmospheres.

Laura Ashley Vinyl Flat Emulsion Paint including this year's versatile new soft colours, is produced with the most up-to-date polymers to give a durable flat finish for interiors. It is available in 1 litre (1.76pints) cans to cover 12sq.metres (127sq.feet), or 2.5litre (.55gallon) cans to cover 30sq.metres (317sq.feet).

Emulsion Paint (2.5litres) **$26.50**
1 litre cans not available in the U.S.A.

Colour	Code	Colour	Code
Stone	*020300*	**White**	*020100*
Cream	*020110*	**Sand**	*020109*
Soft Apricot	*020293*	**Lt.Aquamarine**	*020290*
Light Guava	*020295*	**Soft Rose**	*020292*
Soft Sapphire	*020291*	**Pale Moss**	*020353*
Light Plum	*020347*	**Light Smoke**	*020345*
Light Sage	*020350*	**Lt.Terracotta**	*020294*
Burgundy	*020115*	**Lt.Kingfisher**	*020296*

SATIN GLOSS PAINT

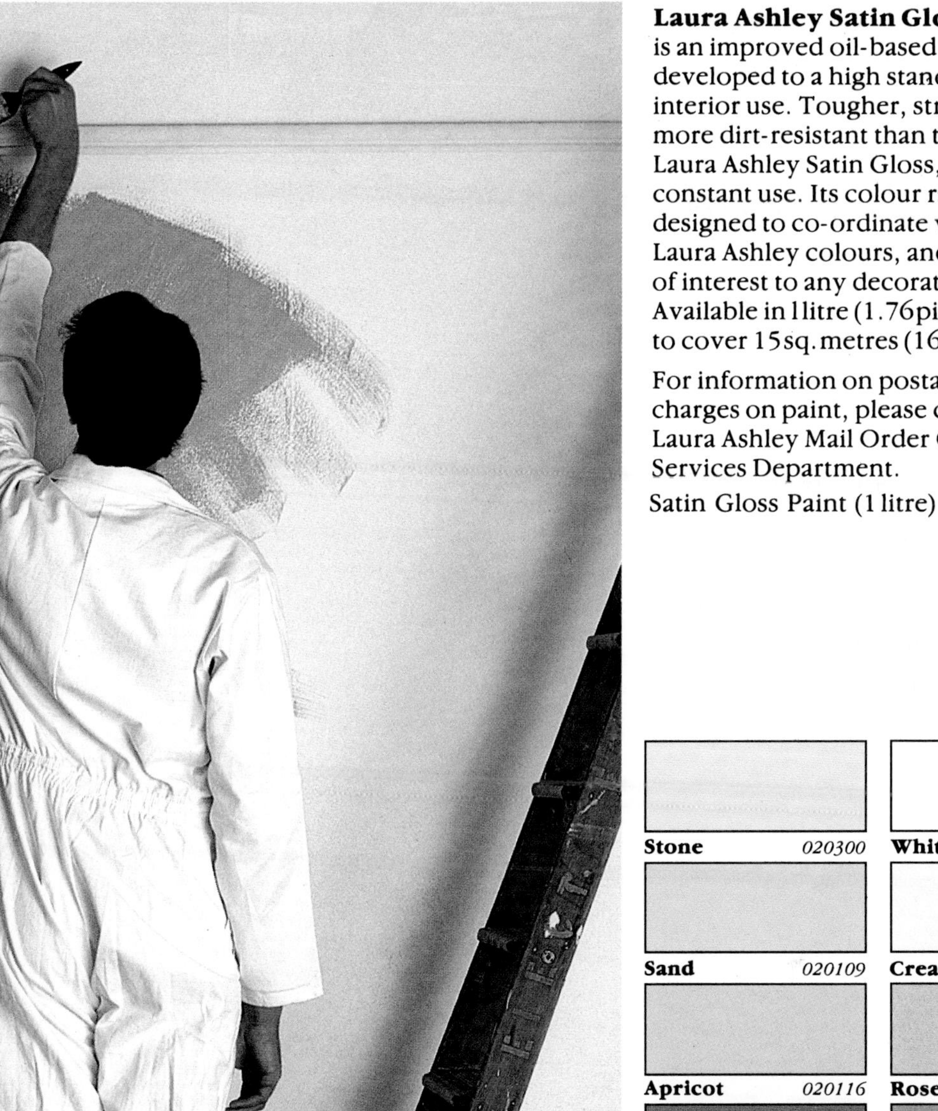

Laura Ashley Satin Gloss Paint is an improved oil-based gloss paint developed to a high standard for interior use. Tougher, stronger and more dirt-resistant than the original Laura Ashley Satin Gloss, for places in constant use. Its colour range is designed to co-ordinate with other Laura Ashley colours, and add a touch of interest to any decorative scheme. Available in 1litre (1.76pints) cans to cover 15sq. metres (160sq. feet).

For information on postal delivery charges on paint, please contact your Laura Ashley Mail Order Customer Services Department.

Satin Gloss Paint (1 litre) **$16.50**

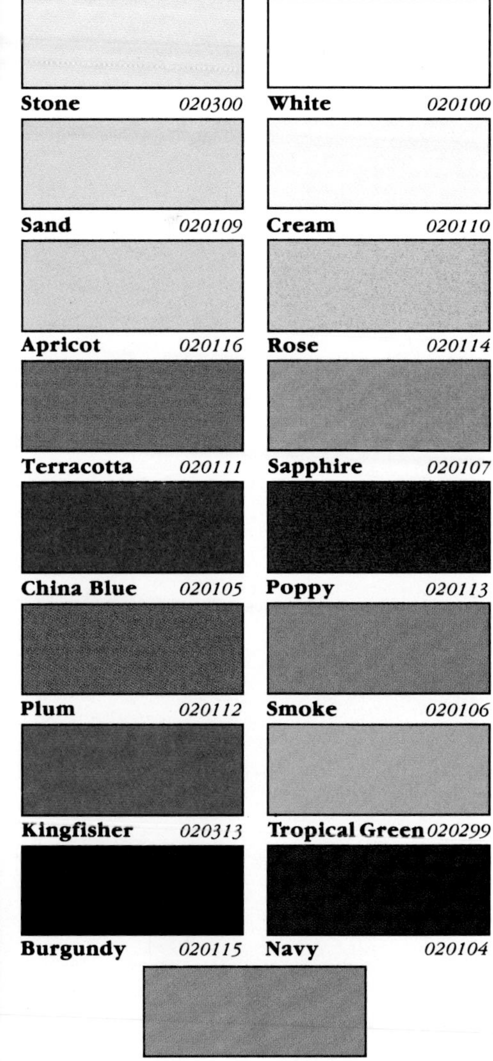

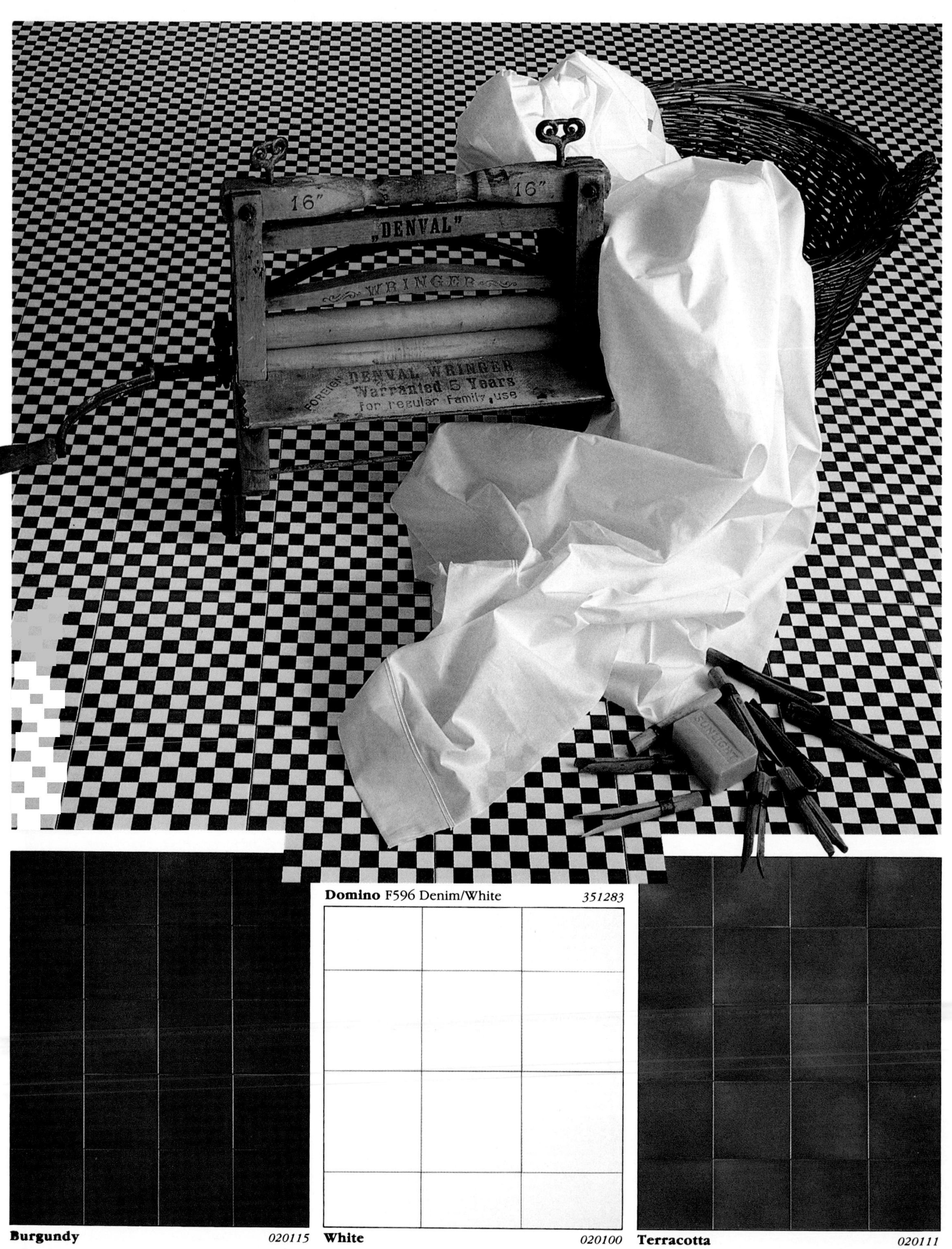

Domino F596 Denim/White *351283*

Burgundy *020115*

White *020100*

Terracotta *020111*

CERAMIC TILES

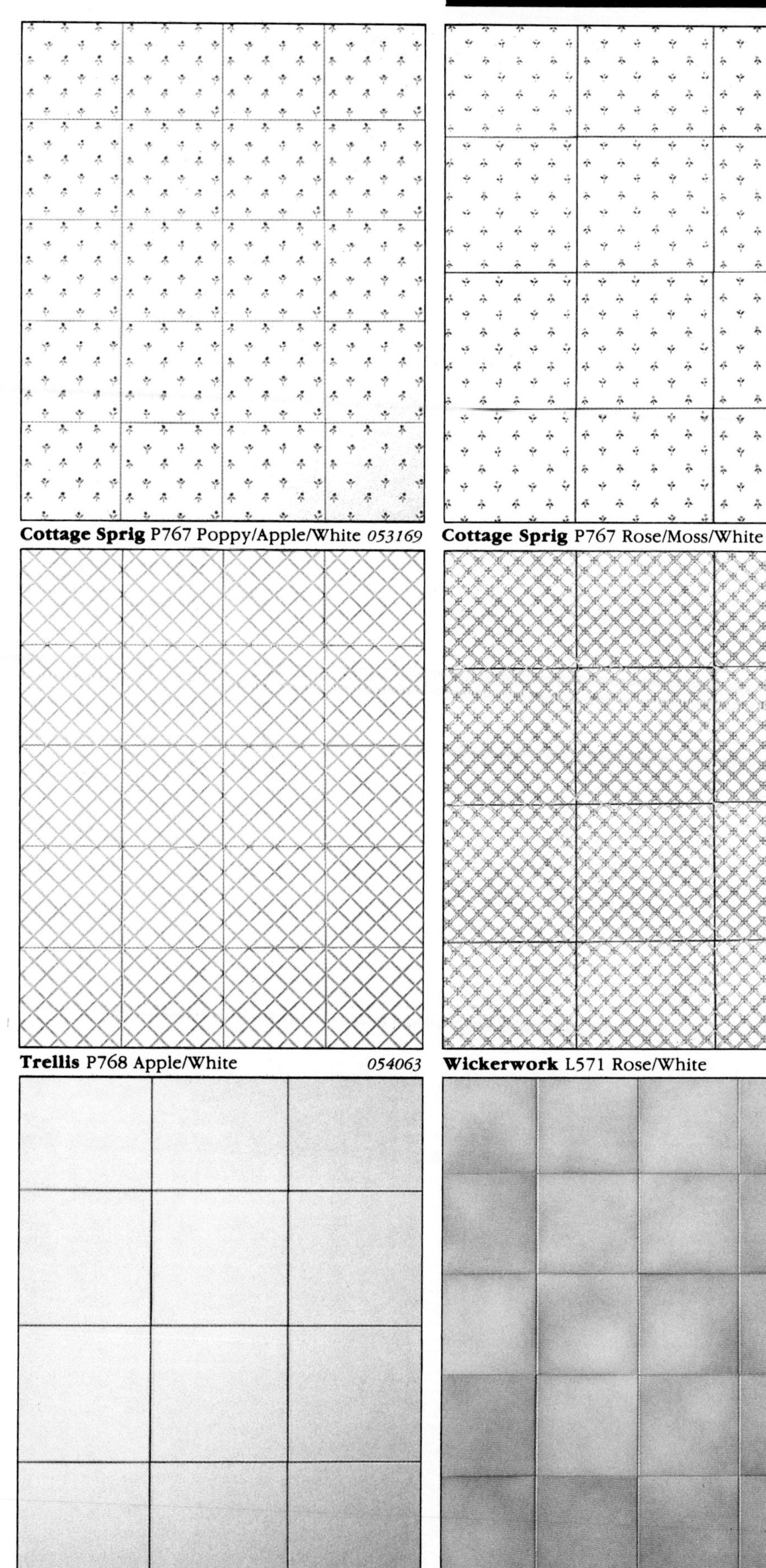

Cottage Sprig P767 Poppy/Apple/White *053169*

Cottage Sprig P767 Rose/Moss/White *053080*

Trellis P768 Apple/White *054063*

Wickerwork L571 Rose/White *041066*

Cream *020110*

Rose *020114*

In a kitchen or bathroom, tiles are indispensable. Whether used as a complete wall covering, or simply as a useful splash-back for a basin, their smart hard-wearing semi-reflective glazed finish is easily wiped clean.

In a more formal room, tiles make an attractive and practical floor covering with a rug, or interesting highlights for existing decoration.

Laura Ashley tiles, made in Italy to a high standard of traditional quality, are available in two sizes and up to twelve different designs, and five coordinating plain colours.
For 1985, the collection includes two bright new geometric patterns – black and white or rose and white squares, and a striking blue and white check.

The large tiles, suitable for walls, and floors not subject to heavy wear, measure 20 × 20cm (8 × 8in) and may require professional advice for application. The small wall tiles 15 × 15cm (6 × 6in) are easier to apply but should not be used on floors. Large tiles are available in packs of 25 to cover one square yard and small tiles in packs of 22 to cover approximately ½ square yard.

For information on postal delivery charges on tiles please contact your Laura Ashley Mail Order Customer Services Department.

Large Tiles

20 × 20cm (8 × 8in) per tile	**$4.00**
20 × 20cm (8 × 8in) per pack	**$87.50**

Small Tiles

15 × 15cm (6 × 6in) per tile	**$2.00**
15 × 5cm (6 × 6in) per pack	**$37.50**

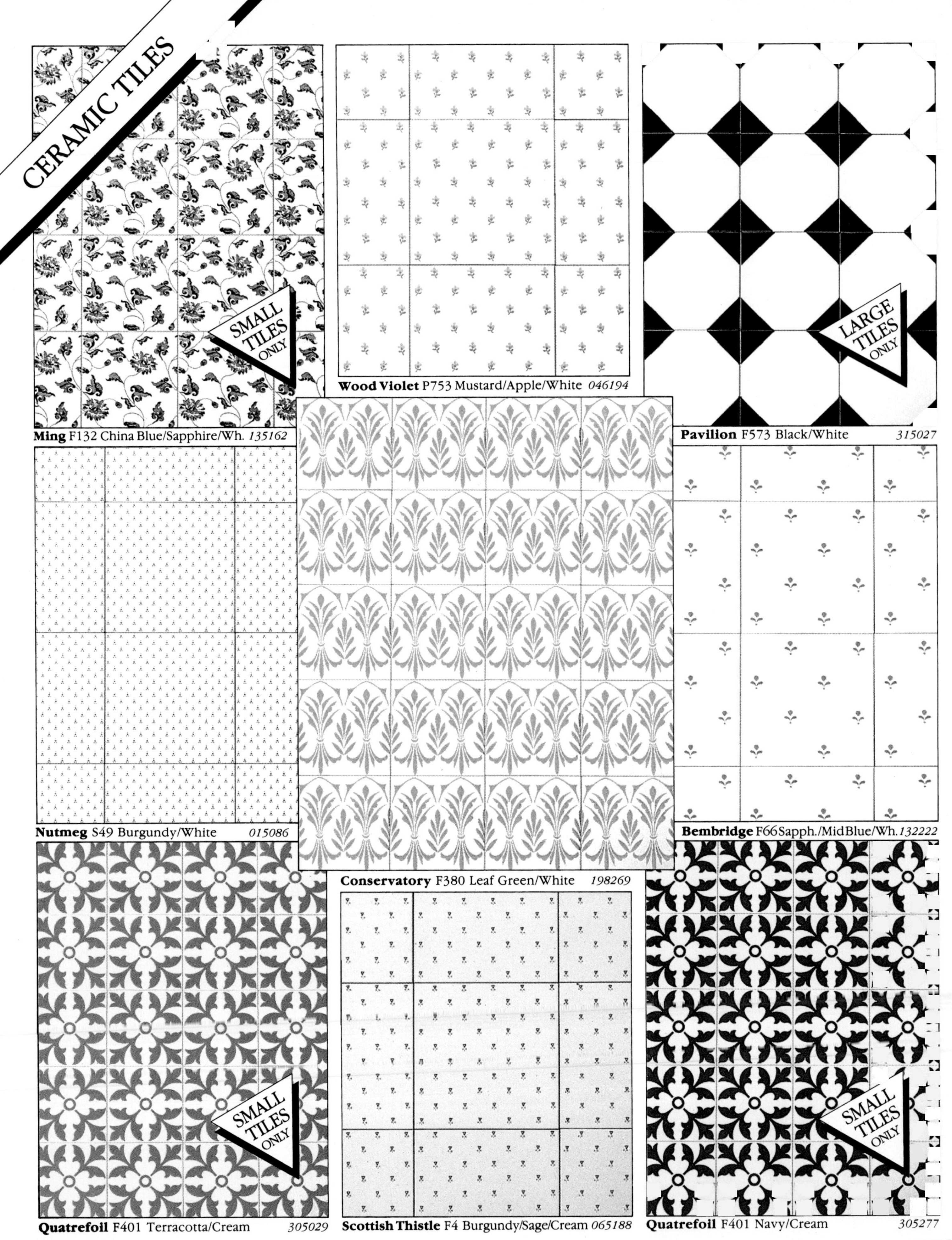

Ming F132 China Blue/Sapphire/Wh. *135162*

Wood Violet P753 Mustard/Apple/White *046194*

Pavilion F573 Black/White *315027*

Nutmeg S49 Burgundy/White *015086*

Conservatory F380 Leaf Green/White *198269*

Bembridge F66Sapph./MidBlue/Wh. *132222*

Quatrefoil F401 Terracotta/Cream *305029*

Scottish Thistle F4 Burgundy/Sage/Cream *065188*

Quatrefoil F401 Navy/Cream *305277*

SMALL TILES ONLY

Pavilion F573 Rose/White *315066*

Terracotta *020111*

Cream *020110*

White *020100*

Rose *020114*

Burgundy *020115*

Tile Borders

These ceramic tiles, new for 1985, can be used with a block of the large 20×20cm tiles to provide an attractive decorative finish.

Available in five plain colourways, size 10×20cm (4 × 8in), in packs of twenty five to cover half a square yard.

For information on postal delivery charges on tiles please contact your Laura Ashley Mail Order Customer Services Dept.

Pack of 25 tile borders
$32.50

Floribunda L577 Multi Apricot *042096*

Paisley F477 Smoke/Kingfisher/Cream *332500*

Petite Fleur R150 Cream/Smoke *026014*

Palmetto F303 Aquamarine/Apricot/White *184268*

Kate F373 Rose/Moss/White *173080*

Rose *020114*

Campion R143 White/Rose *021067*

Paisley F477 Plum/Saddle/Cream *332264*

Nutmeg S49 White/Burgundy *015084*

Wickerwork L571 White/Sapphire *041073*

Wild Clematis S65 Smoke/Cream *004013*

LIGHTING

Finding the right lamp can often be an immensely difficult task, but Laura Ashley has made the search easier with her classically shaped table lamp which features a glazed ceramic base in white or cream, and a crisply pleated shade of 100% cotton fabric. Choose from three sizes and a wide variety of patterns to create rooms that are beautifully co-ordinated or engagingly eclectic. Patterns and color possibilities are indicated opposite and below.

Large Lampshade **$36.00**
Height: 11 ½ in, diameter: 16in

Medium Lampshade **$31.00**
Height: 11 ½ in, diameter: 14in

Small Lampshade **$26.00**
Height: 7 ½ in, diameter: 10in

Large Octagonal Lampbase **$50.00**
Height (base height only): 12 ½ in

Large Rounded Lampbase **$42.50**
Height from base to top of lamp: 24 ¾ in

Medium Rounded Lampbase **$36.50**
Height from base to top of lamp: 21 ¼ in

Small Rounded Lampbase **$32.50**
Ht. from base to top of clip shade: 14 ½ in

Floribunda L577 Multi Sapphire *042195*

Wild Cherry S56 Cream/Plum *003012*

Ming F132 China Blue/Sapphire/White *135162*

Nutmeg S49 Sand/Navy *015019*

Milfoil L570 Cream/Terracotta *040030*

Cornflowers F333 Sapphire Multi Mustard *187485*

DRESSING ROOM COLLECTION

Eight different prints. A lovely way to add colour to any dressing table whether at home or en route.

Sponge Bag **$19.50**
Size: 3½ × 9½ × 11 in
Cosmetic Bag **$16.00**
Size: 2¾ × 6 × 9 in
Small Cosmetic Bag **$15.50**
Size: 1 × 4¼ × 7 in
All in 100% quilted cotton, lined with strong wipeable plasticised cotton and piped in matching plain binding.

Sewing/Jewelry Box **$32.50**
Size: 3 × 8 × 12 in
Beautifully finished in country furnishing cotton, this is for the home dressmaker, or for jewels and trinkets.

Sewing Kit **$12.50**
Size: 4½ × 5 in
The sewing kit contains tape measure, multi-coloured thread plait and pins and needles. 100% quilted cotton.

Tissue Box & Cover **$14.50**
Size: 3 × 5 × 10½ in

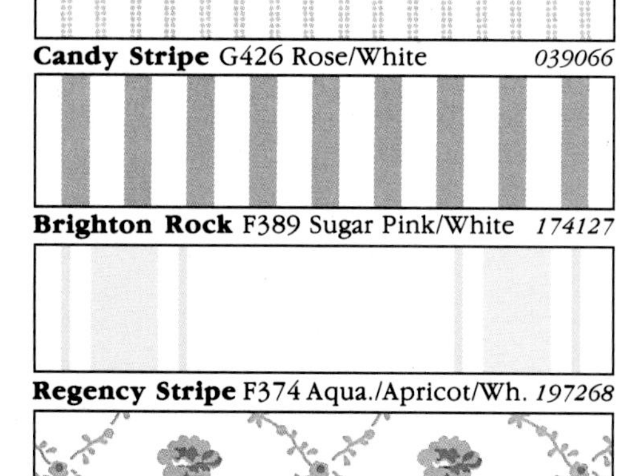

Candy Stripe G426 Rose/White *039066*

Brighton Rock F389 Sugar Pink/White *174127*

Regency Stripe F374 Aqua./Apricot/Wh. *197268*

Kate F373 Rose/Moss/White *173080*

Cornflowers F333 Sapph. Multi Mustard *187485*

Paisley F477 Smoke/Kingfisher/Cream *332500*

Paisley F477 Plum/Saddle/Cream *332264*

Stitchwort F320 Navy/Burgundy/Sand *191261*

DESK COLLECTION

These very pretty fabric-covered frames, photo albums and desk accessories in a choice of six prints make your favorite pictures look even more attractive while providing subtle ways of giving an added accent to any room.

Small Square Frame **$12.50**
Size: 5 × 5 in. Holds 3½ × 3½ in photos.

Medium Single Frame **$13.50**
Size: 5 × 6½ in. Holds 3½ × 5 in photos.

Large Single Frame **$17.50**
Size: 7 × 9 in. Holds 5 × 7 in photos.

Double Folding Frame **$14.50**
Size: 5 × 6½ in closed. Holds two 3½ × 5 in photos.

Desk Note Pad **$15.00**
Size: 7 × 5 in. Holds refillable note pad.

Refill for Note Pad **$5.25**

Photo Album **$37.50**
Size: 12 × 12½ in. With (15) 10 × 12 in magnetic page inserts.

Refills for Photo Album **$8.00**
In packages of five with two extenders.

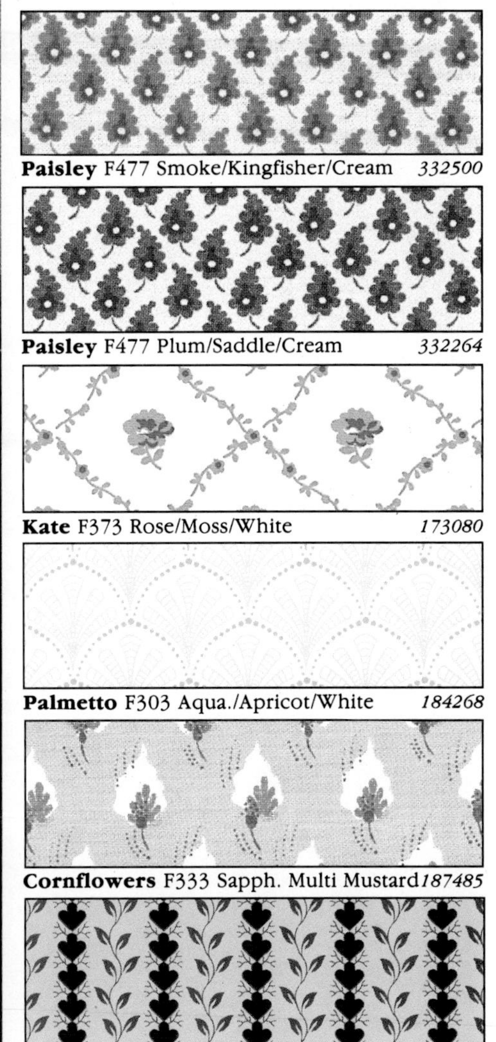

Paisley F477 Smoke/Kingfisher/Cream *332500*

Paisley F477 Plum/Saddle/Cream *332264*

Kate F373 Rose/Moss/White *173080*

Palmetto F303 Aqua./Apricot/White *184268*

Cornflowers F333 Sapph. Multi Mustard *187485*

Stitchwort F320 Navy/Burgundy/Sand *191261*

DINING COLLECTION

1

2

3

4

5

6

Tablecloths were once only for the very rich, serving as a protection for the fine wood of the dining table.
In keeping with this spirit, Laura Ashley has produced a collection of tablecloths, napkins and accessories in a variety of co-ordinating prints and colourways suitable for any occasion.

This year's collection contains three exciting new fabric designs – tablecloths and napkins in a colourful floral bouquet, cosies and place-mats in a delicate cherry and green sprig, and a small square tablecloth in brilliant primary colours. The Harlequin small square tablecloth 84 × 84cm (33 × 33in) is not available in the U.S.A.

Square Tablecloth 132 × 132cm (52 × 52in)	**$22.00**
Rectangular Tablecloth 132 × 178cm (52 × 70in)	**$32.00**
Small Round Tablecloth 178cm (70in) diameter	**$32.00**
Round Tablecloth 228cm (90in) diameter	**$42.00**
Set of Four Napkins 42 × 42cm (16½ × 16½ in)	**$16.00**
Place-Mat 30 × 45cm (12 × 17¾ in)	**$7.00**
Tea-Cosy 24 × 28cm (9½ × 11in)	**$16.50**
Egg-Cosy 10 × 10cm (4 × 4in)	**$5.00**

Shown Opposite – Tablecloth & Napkins:
Morning Parlour
F474 Deep Sapphire Multi White *098497*
Tea-Cosy, Egg-Cosies & Place Mats:
Polly F511 Cherry Multi White *322244*

1. Tablecloth & Napkins:
Dandelion F335 Terracotta/Moss/Cr. *302270*
Tea-Cosy, Egg-Cosies & Place-Mats:
Milfoil L570 Cream/Terracotta *040030*

2. Tablecloth & Napkins:
Mr.Jones F381 Navy/Burgundy/Sand *190261*
Tea-Cosy, Egg-Cosies & Place-Mats:
Nutmeg S49 Sand/Navy *015019*

3. Tablecloth & Napkins:
Cottage Sprig P767 Rose/Moss/White *053080*
Tea-Cosy, Egg-Cosies & Place-Mats:
Cottage Sprig P767 Rose/Moss/White *053080*

4. Tablecloth & Napkins:
Gingham F386 Poppy Multi White *186143*
Tea-Cosy, Egg-Cosies & Place-Mats:
Cottage Sprig P767 Poppy/Apple/Wh. *053169*

5. Tablecloth & Napkins:
Conservatory F380 Leaf Green/White *198269*
Tea-Cosy, Egg-Cosies & Place-Mats:
Nutmeg S49 White/Moss *015017*

6. Small Square Tablecloth:
Harlequin F593 Denim/Tropical Green/White
343448

FRILLED CUSHIONS

Cushions add a luxurious finishing touch to a sofa or armchair, providing the contrast needed to relieve a background design. Originally only found in great houses, cushions still have the look and feel of extravagance, but can now be used as freely as one might wish, being one of the simplest and least expensive ways of creating a feeling of traditional opulence.

Laura Ashley round frilled (34cm/13½in diameter) and square frilled (45cm sq./17½in sq.) cushion covers in 100% cotton are available in a number of versatile prints and colourways and may be purchased separately, or with cushions filled with soft feather pads of the very highest quality.

This year, ten new prints have been introduced to the collection including, for the frilled square cushion covers, the new botanical print in pinks, greens, smokey blues and browns, and a simple rustic blue and white spot.

Round Frilled Cover	**$25.00**
Round Frilled Cover with Pad	**$35.00**
Square Frilled Cover	**$25.00**
Square Frilled Cover with Pad	**$35.00**
Round Pad	**$12.00**
Square Pad	**$12.00**

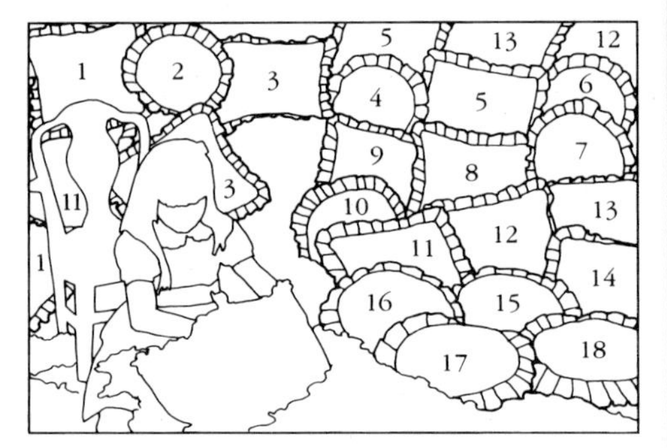

1. **Kew Gardens** F484 Mint Multi White	*090396*
2. **Penelope** F535 Mint Multi White	*095396*
3. **Cricket Stripe** F369 Terracotta/Moss/Cream	*185449*
4. **Dandelion** F335 Terracotta/Moss/Cream	*302270*
5. **Harbour** F490 Kingfisher/Stone	*324255*
6. **Sea Spray** F493 Kingfisher/Stone	*323255*
7. **Stitchwort** F320 Navy/Burgundy/Sand	*191261*
8. **Palmetto** F303 Kingfisher/Burgundy/Cream	*184256*
9. **Riviera** F222 Sapphire/Mustard	*131221*
10. **Cornflowers** F333 Sapphire Multi Mustard	*107485*
11. **Regency Stripe** F374 Aqua./Apricot/White	*197268*
12. **Cricket Stripe** F369 Plum/Saddle/Cream	*185264*
13. **Mr Jones** F381 Navy/Burgundy/Sand	*190261*
14. **Campion** R143 White/Rose	*021067*
15. **Kate** F373 Rose/Moss/White	*173080*
16. **Regency Stripe** F374 Apricot/Aqua./White	*197265*
17. **Paisley** F477 Smoke/Kingfisher/Cream	*332500*
18. **Paisley** F477 Plum/Saddle/Cream	*332264*

PIPED CUSHIONS

Also new to the collection are plain piped square chintz cushion covers in six colourways (40cm sq./15½ in sq.) and two flamboyant new prints on un-frilled square cushion covers (39cm sq./15¼ in sq.), Emma (piped), and Columbine (un-piped). The covers may be washed or dry cleaned.

Piped Cover	**$21.00**
Columbine Cover	**$21.00**
Emma Cover	**$21.00**
Square Cushion Pads	**$12.00**

1. **Tropical Green**	*020299*
2. **Aquamarine**	*020340*
3. **Rose**	*020114*
4. **Poppy**	*020113*
5. **Sapphire**	*020107*
6. **Apricot**	*020116*
7. **Emma** C17 Multi Straw Cream	*517401*
8. **Columbine** F583 Denim Multi White	*338506*

BURLINGTON PATTERNED BEDLINENS

An exclusive range of bedlinen designed for Laura Ashley by Burlington Mills. This season's new collection features bold wide stripes and more masculine prints making it more masculine than ever before and complementing perfectly the small florals for which Laura Ashley has become renowned. All bedlinen is made in easy-care 200 count Cale, a blend of Celanese Fortrel polyester and pure cotton.

TICKING STRIPE

Shown below. The sheer simplicity of the stripe, in pale pink on snowy white, contrasts beautifully with the fresh rosebud pattern shown on the reverse of the comforter and the accessory pillows. Whether the ticking stripe, with its pink piping, is paired with the comforter or on its own, it will surely become one of your favorite designs. Prices are shown below.

BEMBRIDGE

Shown right. Laura Ashley has combined a smart stripe and a naïve stylised stencil sprig design in fresh sapphire blue and pure white to capture the rustic simplicity of primitive native folk art. The two designs join together to create the perfect bedroom atmosphere of inviting calm and tranquility. Prices are shown on page 112.

BURLINGTON TICKING STRIPE PRICE LIST

Fitted Sheets								**Dust Ruffle**	
Twin	$22.50	Full	$28.00	**Shams**		King	$100.00	A full ruffled skirt	
Full	$28.00	Queen	$33.00	Standard	$34.00	**Comforter**		that completes each line	
Queen	$33.00	King	$38.00	King	$39.00	Quilted and filled with		design.	
King	$38.00	California King	$38.00			100% celanese cotton.		Twin	$56.00
California King	$38.00			**Duvet Cover**		Twin	$105.00	Full	$62.00
		Pillows Cases (per pair)		Twin	$67.00	Full	$125.00	Queen	$67.00
Flat Sheets		Standard	$22.50	Full	$78.00	Queen	$145.00	King	$77.00
Twin	$22.50	King	$25.00	Queen	$89.00	King	$175.00	California King	$77.00

G. POTTS

PALMETTO

Shown far left. The cool sunlight of a summer at the seashore. Bold awning stripes and a pretty palm-floral motif in beautifully relaxing tones of sun-bleached apricot and aquamarine. Prices are shown on page 112.

CASTLEBERRY

Shown left. Recall the grace and charm of a turn-of-the-century summer complete with porch swings and cool sweeping verandahs with our own Castleberry, a design which combines tiny rose and moss-green buds with delicate vines of tulips, all on a fresh white ground. Prices are shown on page 112.

KENSINGTON

Shown left. A crisp clean pattern of smoke blue on cream that combines delicate forget-me-nots with an elegant Victorian border. Prices are shown on page 112.

NUTMEG

Shown on the following page. Refreshingly urbane and very sophisticated. New life for an ancient motif now used on a border atop a deep, masculine navy blue, broken up by tiny sprig-like sand coloured dots. Prices are shown on page 112.

NUTMEG – Description on previous page. Prices are given below.

BURLINGTON PATTERNED BEDLINEN PRICE LIST

Sheets Flat or Fitted	
Twin	$23.50
Full	$30.00
Queen	$36.00
King	$42.00
California King	$42.00
Pillow Cases (per pair)	
Standard	$30.00
King	$32.50

Shams	
Standard	$40.00
King	$48.00
Duvet Covers*	
Twin	$78.00
Full	$90.00
Queen	$105.00
King	$110.00

* Not available in Nutmeg, Palmetto and Bembridge.

Dust Ruffle
A full ruffled skirt that completes each design.

Dust Ruffle	
Twin	$65.00
Full	$75.00
Queen	$84.00
King	$94.00
California King	$94.00

Comforter
Quilted comforter filled with 100% Celanese Fortrel polyester

Comforter	
Twin	$130.00
Full	$155.00
Queen	$185.00
King	$222.00

Pillows	
Sq. Decorative	$30.00
Rd. Decorative	$30.00
Head Roll	$30.00
Tablelinen	
Table Round*	$52.00
Tablecloth Ensem.*	$55.00

* Not available in Kensington & Castleberry.

BURLINGTON SOLID BEDLINENS

Rose *020114*

Sapphire *020107*

Plum *020112*

Smoke *020106*

Laura Ashley's newest introduction: a range of bedlinen in four glorious shades designed especially to co-ordinate with her patterned collections. Choose from rose, sapphire, plum or smoke and create a room which is calm and inviting. All are made of '200 Cale', a 50/50 blend of combed cotton and Celanese Fortrel polyester.

BURLINGTON SOLID BEDLINEN PRICE LIST

Fitted Sheets								**Dust Ruffle**	
Twin	$17.50	Queen	$30.50	King	$22.50	Full	$154.00	A full ruffled skirt that	
Full	$22.50	King	$37.50	**Shams**	$36.00	Queen	$180.00	completes each design.	
Queen	$30.50	**Pillows**		Standard	$34.00	King	$215.00	Twin	$52.00
King	$37.50	Sq. Decorative	$30.00	King Sham	$46.00	**Duvet Covers**		Full	$59.00
California King	$37.50	Rd. Decorative	$30.00	**Comforter**		Twin	$78.00	Queen	$66.00
Flat Sheets		Head Roll	$30.00	Quilted and filled with		Full	$90.00	King & Cal. King	$78.00
Twin	$17.50	**Pillow Cases** (per pair)		100% Celanese polyester		Queen	$105.00	Table Round	$55.00
Queen	$22.50	Standard	$20.00	Twin	$128.00	King	$110.00	Table Ensemble	$60.00

PATCHWORK QUILTS & PATCHWORK PIECES

Patchwork Quilts
Hand-made in Wales, Laura Ashley patchwork quilts add colour and variety to any bedroom, used either to blend into an existing colour scheme, or as interesting contrast. Available in the five co-ordinating colourways shown above.

Single Patchwork Quilt	**$195.00**
Double Patchwork Quilt	**$310.00**

Rose	*020114*
Plum	*020112*
Sapphire	*020107*
Smoke	*020106*
Poppy	*020113*

Patchwork Pieces
For the enterprising seamstress, the same square patchwork pieces used in Laura Ashley quilts are available in a selection of different colour combined packs.

Each pack contains approximately 100 × 12 cm (4¾ in) squares to cover a minimum of 1sq. yard.
$10.00 per pack

Also available are hexagonal patchwork pieces, in similar colour co-ordinated packs. Each pack contains approx. 120 × 10cm (4in) width hexagons to cover a minimum of 1 square yard.
$10.00 per pack

Rose	*020114*
Plum	*020112*
Sapphire	*020107*
Smoke	*020106*
Poppy	*020113*
Moss	*020102*
Navy	*020104*
China Blue	*020105*
Terracotta	*020111*
Burgundy	*020115*

Shower Curtain Kit

A useful new addition to the range of accessories is this 180cmsq. (70in) shower curtain kit.

Made from water-resistant plain white nylon, with simple metal eyelets, it forms the perfect lining to hang inside a curtain made from country furnishing cotton, creating an attractive shower curtain to co-ordinate perfectly with the rest of your bathroom decoration.

The shower curtain kit comes complete with additional eyelets and a hole-punch to assist you in fitting your choice of fabric. Not available in the U.S.A.

Lace Panels

As a refreshing alternative to curtains for privacy, Laura Ashley presents these attractive Nottingham lace panels, made on the original Jacquard looms, with a stylised border surrounding a central reserve of swags and bows. Backed with a plain material they make a light and different variation on draw curtains. Each panel, sold individually, measures 152 × 228cm (60 × 90in) and has an open hem at the top for hanging. Available in ivory (*020125*) and white (*020100*).
$50.00

Chipboard Tables

A round table kit, designed for use as a basic structure to be covered with a Laura Ashley tablecloth. The 'instant' table has an uncomplicated slot assembly and can be dismantled flat for easy storage.

Small Chipboard Table **$40.00**
Diam.: 53cm (21in). Ht.: 61cm (24in).

Large Chipboard Table **$55.00**
Diam: 79cm (31in). Ht: 72cm (28in)

Lining Fabric

Pure cotton lining fabric. For details see Mail Order insert. **$4.50** per yard.

Roller Blind Kit

The simple, classic design perfect for kitchens, bathrooms and the less formal rooms of the house. An easy to assemble roller blind kit including an aluminium roller, fabric stiffener, fixing brackets and wooden pull. In fact everything needed apart from the fabric itself. The kits are available in three sizes to cover widths up to 3, 4, and 6feet. 3feet **$24.00**, 4feet **$30.00**, 6feet **$40.00**.

1
2 3

UPHOLSTERED FURNITURE

4

5

The new Laura Ashley Furniture Collection with eight way hand-tied coil construction.

An entirely new collection of upholstered furniture has been designed by Laura Ashley to reflect the range and sophistication of this year's Home Furnishing Collection. This furniture is constructed to exacting standards by Bridgeford, the renowned upholstered furniture division of Henredon.

You can choose any of our fabrics in any of the patterns available in this catalog.

Visit one of our shops in the U.S. or simply call our toll free number (1-800-367-2000). We'll help you choose your furniture and can have it delivered in the Continental United States at a very reasonable cost.

1. **Milford Sofa**

Width 86½ in, depth 36in, height 33¼ in
Arm height 29in

Country furnishing cotton	**$1300**
Chintz	**$1585**
Drawingrm/Upholstery fabric	**$1870**

Kent Chair

Width 31in, depth 33¼ in, height 32½ in
Arm height 25in

Country furnishing cotton	**$740**
Chintz	**$950**
Drawingrm/Upholstery fabric	**$1160**

2. **Cambria Loveseat**

Width 65in, depth 35in, height 31¼ in
Arm height 26in

Country furnishing cotton	**$1190**
Chintz	**$1475**
Drawingrm/Upholstery fabric	**$1760**

3. **Cambria Chair**

Width 41in, depth 33¾ in, height 30in
Arm height 25¾ in

Country furnishing cotton	**$825**
Chintz	**$1035**
Drawingrm/Upholstery fabric	**$1245**

4. **Tudor Chair**

Width 32¼ in, depth 33½ in, height 35in
Arm height 25in

Country furnishing cotton	**$825**
Chintz	**$1035**
Drawingrm/Upholstery fabric	**$1245**

5. **Carlisle Loveseat**

Width 65in, depth 36¾ in, height 32¾ in
Arm height 24in

Country furnishing cotton	**$1670**
Chintz	**$1950**
Drawingrm/Upholstery fabric	**$2230**

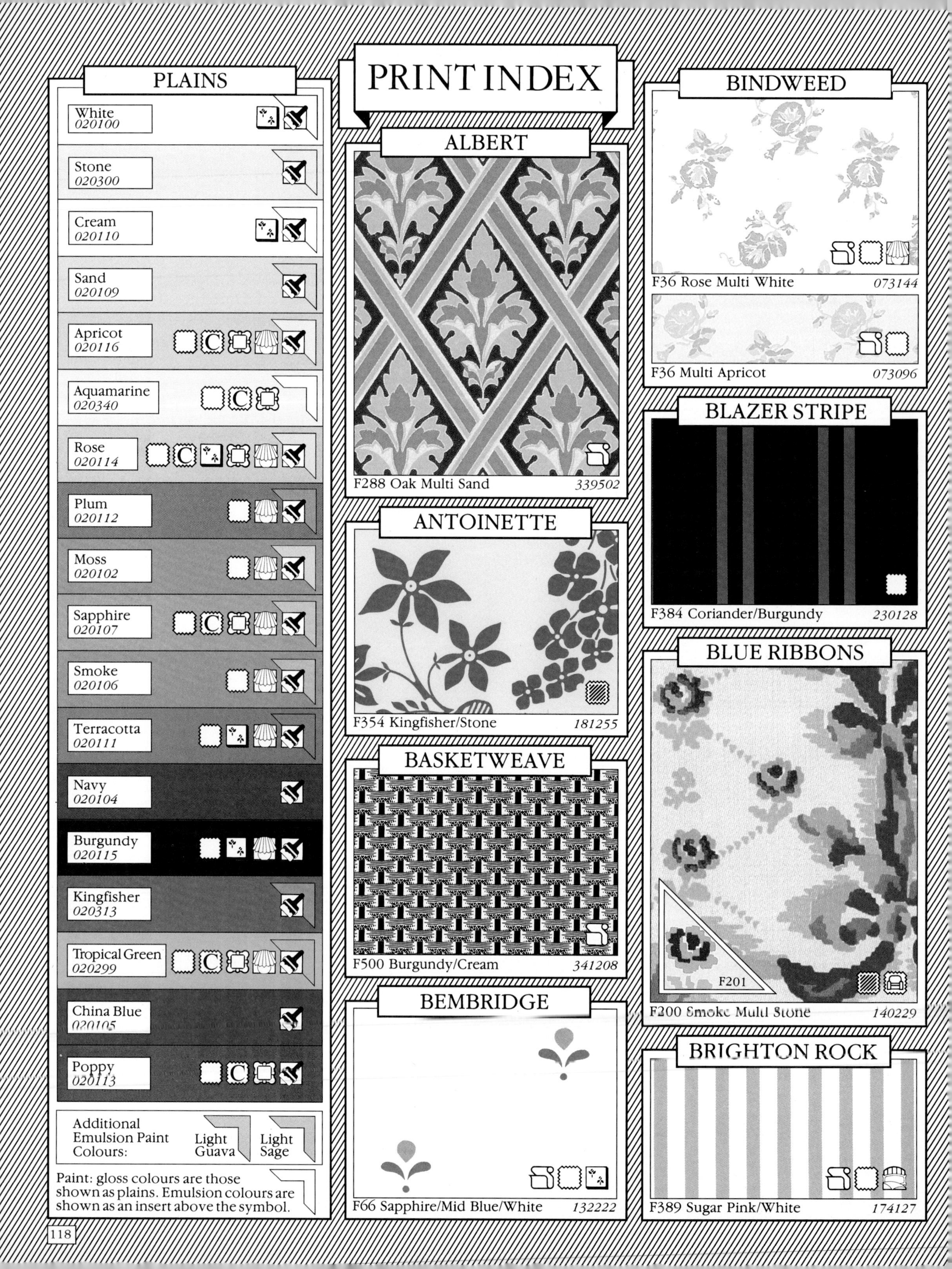

PRINT INDEX

PLAINS

Colour	Code
White	020100
Stone	020300
Cream	020110
Sand	020109
Apricot	020116
Aquamarine	020340
Rose	020114
Plum	020112
Moss	020102
Sapphire	020107
Smoke	020106
Terracotta	020111
Navy	020104
Burgundy	020115
Kingfisher	020313
Tropical Green	020299
China Blue	020105
Poppy	020113

Additional Emulsion Paint Colours: Light Guava, Light Sage

Paint: gloss colours are those shown as plains. Emulsion colours are shown as an insert above the symbol.

ALBERT

F288 Oak Multi Sand *339502*

ANTOINETTE

F354 Kingfisher/Stone *181255*

BASKETWEAVE

F500 Burgundy/Cream *341208*

BEMBRIDGE

F66 Sapphire/Mid Blue/White *132222*

BINDWEED

F36 Rose Multi White *073144*

F36 Multi Apricot *073096*

BLAZER STRIPE

F384 Coriander/Burgundy *230128*

BLUE RIBBONS

F201

F200 Smoke Multi Stone *140229*

BRIGHTON ROCK

F389 Sugar Pink/White *174127*

PRINT INDEX

CAMPION

R143 White/Sapphire *021073*

R143 Sapphire/White *021072*

R143 White/Rose *021067*

R143 Rose/White *021066*

CANDY STRIPE

G426 Rose/White *039066*

G426 Sapphire/White *039072*

G426 Navy/Sand *039020*

CLARISSA

F45 Apricot Multi White *076146*

CLIFTON CASTLE

F353 Sand/Navy *183019*

F353 Cream/Sand *183129*

F353 Cream/Plum *183012*

CLOVER

F43 Rose/White *075066*

F43 Sapphire/White *075072*

CONSERVATORY

F380 Leaf Green/White *198269*

CONVOLVULUS

L610 Multi Rose *060459*

CORDELIA

F537 Multi Stone *328397*

CORNFLOWERS

F333 Sapphire Multi Mustard *187485*

COTTAGE SPRIG

P767 Rose/Moss/White *053080*

P767 Poppy/Apple/White *053169*

P767 China Blue/Apple/White *053171*

COTTON SEED

P754 Sky Blue Multi White *047381*

PRINT INDEX

COUNTRY ROSES

F430 Rose Multi White *089144*

CRICKET STRIPE

F369 Sand/Navy/Cream *185262*

F369 Terracotta/Moss/Cream *185449*

F369 Plum/Saddle/Cream *185264*

F369 Sapphire/China Blue/White *185258*

DAMASK

F526 Kingfisher/Smoke *326281*

F526 Dark Green/Mid Green *326499*

DANDELION

F335 Terracotta/Moss/Cream *302270*

F335 Plum/Sage/Cream *302447*

F335 Denim/Tropical Green/White *302448*

DEAUVILLE

F559 Oak Multi Stone *337509*

DELHI

F329 Multi Salmon *303386*

EDWARD

F456 Kingfisher/Stone *325255*

EMMA

C17 Multi Guava/Stone *517400*

C17 Multi Straw/Cream *517401*

EMMELINE

F127 Sand Multi White *147139*

EMPEROR

F210 Navy Multi Stone *145231*

F210 Terracotta Multi Cream *145233*

ENGLISH GARDEN

F367 Taupe Multi White *178486*

PRINT INDEX

FAVORITA
F206 Dark Green Multi Sand 144230
F206 Navy Multi Sand 144480
FLORENTINA
F358 Burgundy Multi Stone 192481
F358 Dark Green Multi Stone 192496
FUCHSIAS
A28 Rose Multi Cream 157156
FLORIBUNDA
L577 Multi Apricot 042096
L577 Multi Poppy 042094
L577 Multi White 042242
L577 Multi Sapphire 042195
L577 Multi China Blue 042093
GARLANDS
F340 Rose Multi Stone 177478
GOTHIC TRELLIS
F352 Multi Sand 194234
HAMILTON
F544
C
F505 Terracotta Multi Cream 092233
GRAPES
F62 Smoke Multi Cream 158247
GINGHAM
F386 Poppy Multi White 186143
F386 Kingfisher Multi Cream 186498
HARBOUR
F490 Kingfisher/Stone 324255

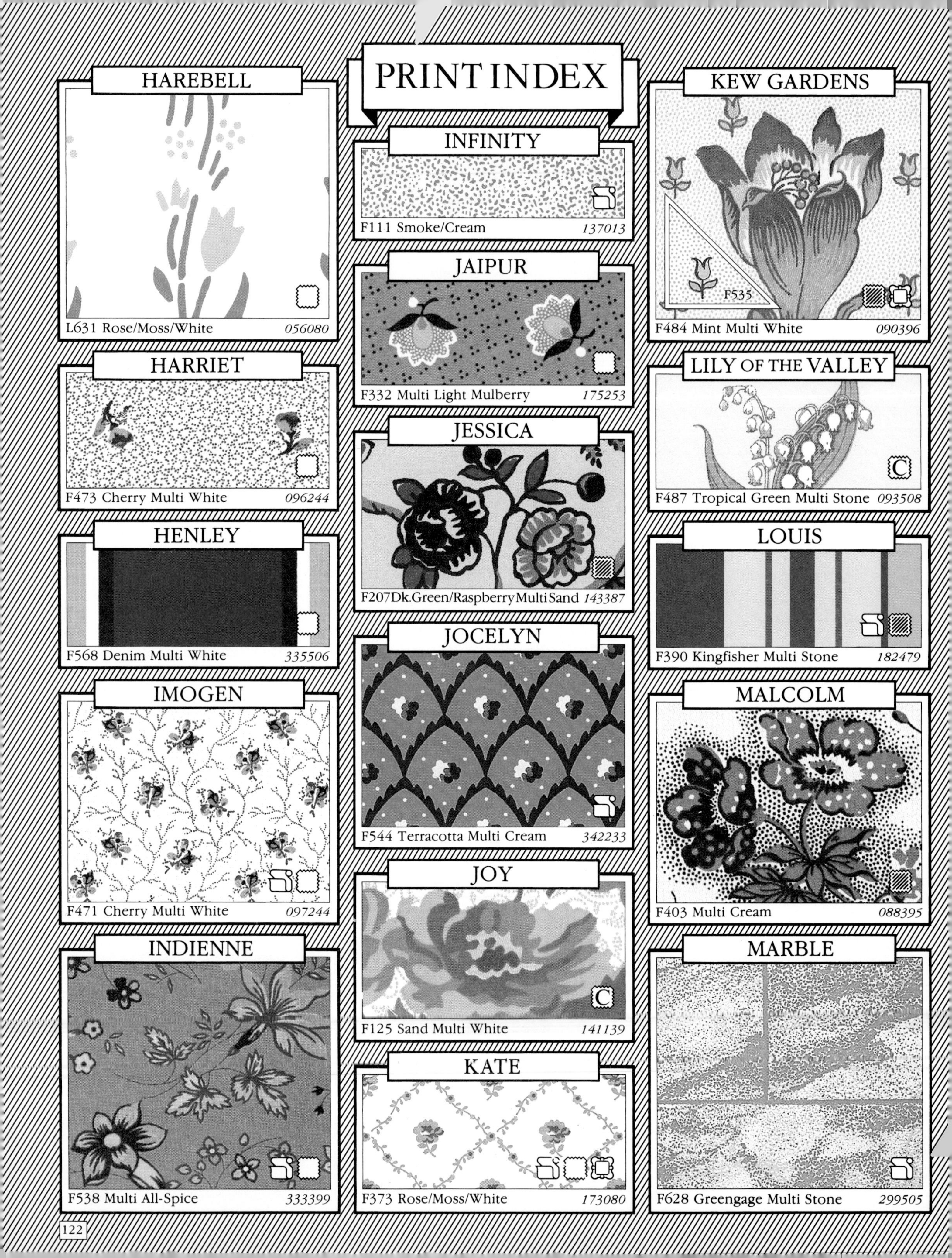

PRINT INDEX

HAREBELL
L631 Rose/Moss/White 056080

HARRIET
F473 Cherry Multi White 096244

HENLEY
F568 Denim Multi White 335506

IMOGEN
F471 Cherry Multi White 097244

INDIENNE
F538 Multi All-Spice 333399

INFINITY
F111 Smoke/Cream 137013

JAIPUR
F332 Multi Light Mulberry 175253

JESSICA
F207Dk.Green/RaspberryMultiSand 143387

JOCELYN
F544 Terracotta Multi Cream 342233

JOY
F125 Sand Multi White 141139

KATE
F373 Rose/Moss/White 173080

KEW GARDENS
F535

F484 Mint Multi White 090396

LILY OF THE VALLEY
F487 Tropical Green Multi Stone 093508

LOUIS
F390 Kingfisher Multi Stone 182479

MALCOLM
F403 Multi Cream 088395

MARBLE
F628 Greengage Multi Stone 299505

PRINT INDEX

MARQUEE
F556 Tropical Green/White *334274*

MARY ANN
F341 Rose/Sky Blue Multi White *172477*

MEADOW FLOWERS
F42 Poppy Multi White *078143*

MICHAELMAS
P768
P769 Burgundy/Sand/White *055185*
P769 Plum/Sand/Cream *055223*

MIDSUMMER
F40 Mustard Multi White *074148*

MILFOIL
L570 Cream/Terracotta *040030*

MING
F132 China Blue/Sapphire/White *135162*

MORNING PARLOUR
F511
F474 Deep Sapphire Multi White *098497*

MR. JONES
F381 Navy/Burgundy/Sand *190261*

NUTMEG
S49 Navy/Sand *015020*
S49 Sand/Navy *015019*
S49 White/Sand *015068*
S49 Burgundy/White *015086*
S49 White/Burgundy *015084*
S49 White/China Blue *015091*
S49 Moss/White *015024*
S49 Sage/Cream *015032*
S49 Plum/Cream *015011*
S49 Saddle/Sand *015002*
S49 White/Moss *015017*
S49 Cream/Sage *015033*
S49 Cream/Plum *015012*

PRINT INDEX

PAISLEY

F477 Smoke/Kingfisher/Cream 332500

F477 Plum/Saddle/Cream 332264

PAISLEY STRIPE

F351 Burgundy/Navy/Stone 188259

PALMETTO

F303 Rose/Moss/White 184080

F303 Aquamarine/Apricot/White 184268

F303 Kingfisher/Burgundy/Cream 184256

F303 Apricot/Aqua./Apricot Wash 18426[illegible]

F303 Sage/Cherry/White 184273

F303 Dark Green/Raspberry/Sand 184263

PARAPET

F378 Taupe/White 180130

PENELOPE

F535 Mint Multi White 095396

PERGOLA

F392 Terracotta Multi Cream 301233

PERIWINKLE

F5

F6 Sky Blue Multi White 067381

POLLY

F511 Cherry Multi White 322244

PONDICHERRY

F339 Light Sage Multi White 304484

POONA

F328 Leaf Green/Raspberry/White 176254

PETITE FLEUR

R150 Terracotta/Cream 026029

R150 Smoke/Cream 026013

R150 Cream/Smoke 026014

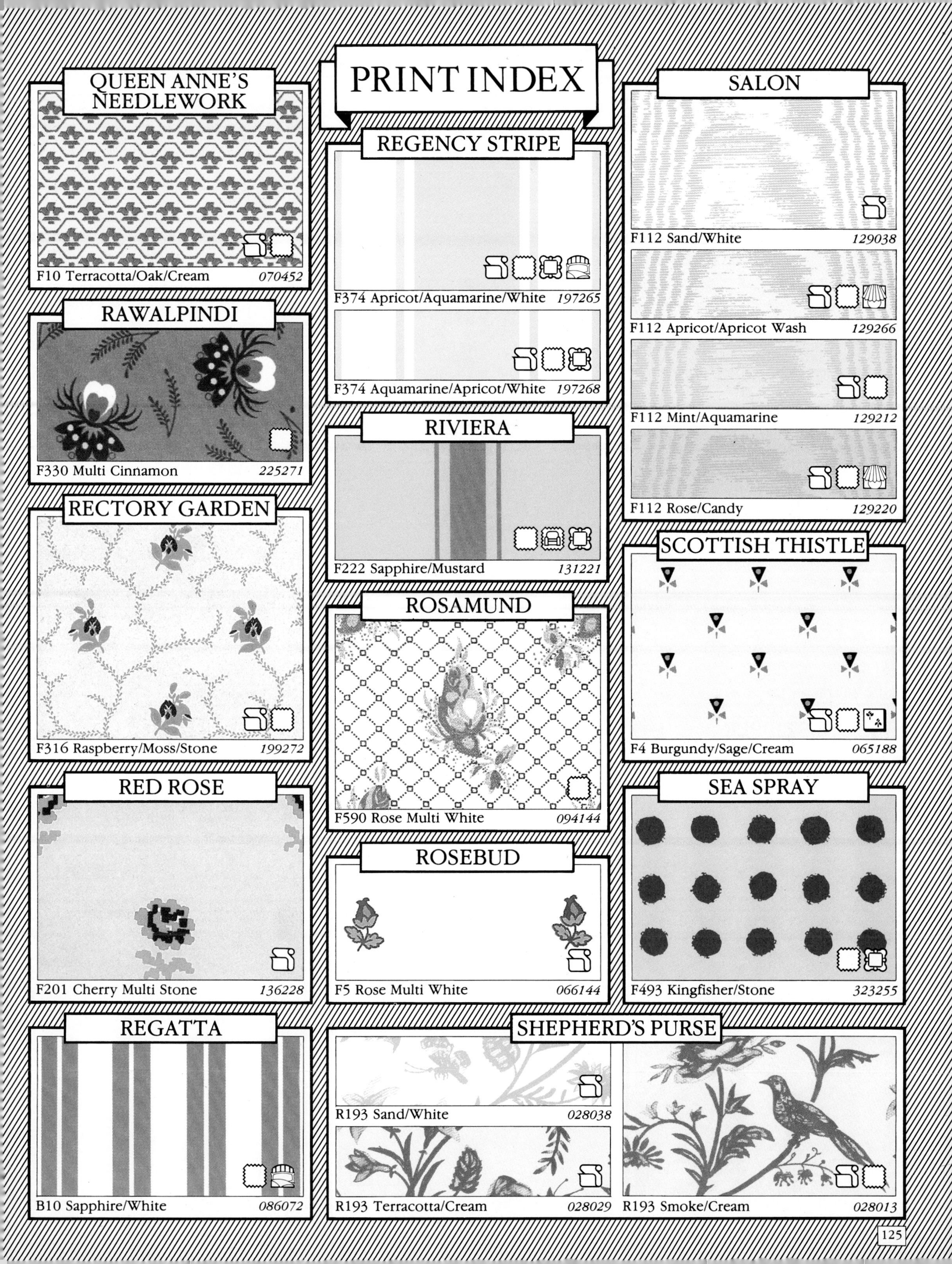
PRINT INDEX
QUEEN ANNE'S NEEDLEWORK
F10 Terracotta/Oak/Cream 070452
RAWALPINDI
F330 Multi Cinnamon 225271
RECTORY GARDEN
F316 Raspberry/Moss/Stone 199272
RED ROSE
F201 Cherry Multi Stone 136228
REGATTA
B10 Sapphire/White 086072
REGENCY STRIPE
F374 Apricot/Aquamarine/White 197265
F374 Aquamarine/Apricot/White 197268
RIVIERA
F222 Sapphire/Mustard 131221
ROSAMUND
F590 Rose Multi White 094144
ROSEBUD
F5 Rose Multi White 066144
SALON
F112 Sand/White 129038
F112 Apricot/Apricot Wash 129266
F112 Mint/Aquamarine 129212
F112 Rose/Candy 129220
SCOTTISH THISTLE
F4 Burgundy/Sage/Cream 065188
SEA SPRAY
F493 Kingfisher/Stone 323255
SHEPHERD'S PURSE
R193 Sand/White 028038
R193 Terracotta/Cream 028029
R193 Smoke/Cream 028013

PRINT INDEX

SIMLA
F516 Multi All-Spice 331399
F516 Multi Terracotta 331398

SOPHIE
F614 Multi Straw/Cream 352401

STIPPLE
F119 Apricot/Primrose 128241

STITCHWORT
F320 Navy/Burgundy/Sand 191261

SUMMERTIME
F557 Multi Poppy 336094

SWEETBRIAR
F388 Rose Multi White 179144

TRELLIS
P768 Sand/Cream 054210
P768 Sand/White 054038
P768 Terracotta/Cream 054029
P768 Mustard/White 054005
P768 Apricot/Apricot Wash 054266
P768 Apple/White 054063

TAPESTRY
F64 Multi Burgundy 156243

TREFOIL
P752 White/Mustard 045001

TULIPS
F488 Multi Stone 327397

VENETIA
F99 Burgundy/Gold 146232

PRINT INDEX
WHITE BOWER
F364 Dark Green Multi Cream 195482
WICKERWORK
L571 White/Sand 041068
L571 Sand/White 041038
L571 White/Sapphire 041073
L571 Sapphire/White 041072
L571 White/Rose 041067
L571 Rose/White 041066
L571 Cream/Sage 041033
L571 Sage/Cream 041032
WILD CHERRY
S56 Smoke/Cream 003013
S56 Cream/Smoke 003014
S56 Sage/Cream 003032
S56 Cream/Plum 003012
S56 Terracotta/Cream 003029
WILD CLEMATIS
S65 Cream/Plum 004012
S65 Plum/Cream 004011
S65 Cream/Smoke 004014
S65 Smoke/Cream 004013
S65 White/Moss 004017
S65 Moss/White 004024
WILD DAMSON
F344 Burgundy/Cream 193208
WIND SPRAY
P784 Sapphire Multi White 057137
WOOD VIOLET
P753 Terracotta/Moss/Cream 046270
P753 Mustard/Apple/White 046194
P753 Rose/Moss/White 046080
P753 Sapphire/Apple/White 046190

INTERIOR DESIGN SERVICE

Our new Interior Design Service can help you realize your personal concept of the ideal Laura Ashley environment.

The Laura Ashley Design Service offers: design consultation on one item, one room, or your whole house, with access to Laura Ashley's complete product line.

This special in-home service is available only through our New York, San Francisco and Boston Interior Design Offices. For additional information or an appointment call:

New York
(212) 517-3772

San Francisco
(415) 788-0796

Boston
(617) 424-6808

Special Notice:
For a fine example of Laura Ashley Design Services, see the Laura Ashley house at the spectacular White Cliffs development near Plymouth, Mass. Call our Boston office for information after March 1st.

LAURA ASHLEY CLOTHES COLLECTION

Laura Ashley means fashion
for you as well as your home.
The Clothes Collection features
elegant gowns, sophisticated tweeds
and the grace and simplicity of her
floral prints on blouses, skirts
and accessories.
There is an emphasis on
natural fabrics and
classic styling.

If you or a friend would
like to receive our seasonal
fashion catalogs four times
throughout the year, fill
out the coupon below and
send $2.00 for each
subscription to:

Laura Ashley Inc.,
Department 866,
Box 5308 Melville,
N.Y. 11747.

MADE TO MEASURE CURTAIN & BLIND SERVICE

Individually finished furnishings add a professional touch to any decorative scheme. Laura Ashley are pleased to offer a unique Made to Measure service in plain and frilled curtains and Roman and Festoon blinds. Our years of experience in interior design and intricate sewing, combined with first class workmanship and a rigid quality control, ensure a high standard in every aspect of these exclusive services.

Curtains
Designed for a particular window, Made to Measure curtains immediately seem a timeless part of any room. The curtains, expertly finished to the customer's exact requirements are available either plain or frilled, in country furnishing cotton, chintz, or drawing room fabric, each fully lined in white or cream satinised lining fabric. A wide variety of prints and colourways ensures that they will blend easily with any existing decoration.
Each pair of curtains individually hand-finished, thus maintaining a strictly personal character along with a high standard of craftsmanship. An 8cm-deep pocket pencil-pleat heading tape allows the curtains to be fitted very close to the ceiling if so required, while each hem is separately turned to a depth of 6cm. Frilled curtains have a 9cm wide double-sided frill sewn in along the leading edge.

Curtain tie-backs
Pairs of tie-backs are available either to match or co-ordinate with curtains. Stiffened to give a smart appearance, they are neatly trimmed in a plain piping.

Shown above – Roman Blind and Wallpaper: **Marquee**, Tropical Green/White.

Shown right – Festoon Blind, Curtains and Tie-backs: **Marquee**, Tropical Green/White.

Blinds
The treatment of windows can completely alter the look of a room or a whole house. While traditional curtains provide an attractive frame for a light source, blinds, used either on their own or with curtains, allow one to control the amount of light let in, subtly altering the atmosphere according to one's mood.

Festoon Blinds
Popular since the eighteenth century, festoon blinds are in reality a form of curtain reefed up on cords in flamboyant swags, to be let down at night. During the day the elegant cascades of fine cloth hang down at regular intervals to cover part of the window, providing a relaxed contrast to the lines of curtains and woodwork. Used on their own, they soften the starkness of a large window and give any room an atmosphere of tranquility. The frilled blinds are available in country furnishing cotton, chintz and drawing room fabric. Each blind is weighted, fully lined in white or cream satinised lining fabric, and has a 7cm-deep pencil-pleat heading and 9cm deep piped frill sewn into the bottom edge. Fittings supplied with the blinds – head rails, brackets, hooks and gliders – are manufactured for Laura Ashley using high grade nylon and precision engineered aluminium. The simple raising mechanism is operated by a fine cord with a brass pull, while an advanced ratchet system allows the blind to be secured at any level.

Roman Blinds
More formal than a conventional roller blind, and suitable for a fully decorated room, but without the feminine flamboyance of a festoon, the new Roman blind is both a traditional and functional way of decorating a window. When raised it offers a delicate concertina-like effect, hanging 25cm from the top of the window. Lowered, it fits neatly into the exact area of the window to give any room a feeling of order and classic proportion. The blinds are available in country furnishing cotton, chintz and drawing room fabric. Fully lined in white or cream satinised lining fabric, they are easily detached from the rail to make cleaning as simple as possible. Fittings supplied with the blinds – head rails and brackets – are manufactured for Laura Ashley using high grade nylon and precision engineered aluminium.
The simple raising mechanism is operated by a fine cord with a brass pull, while the same successful advanced ratchet system as used on Laura Ashley festoon blinds allows the blind to be secured at any level.

HOW TO ORDER

CURTAINS

1. Choose the design, colourway and fabric from those shown in the print index on pages 116-125 of this catalog.

2. Measure the width of your curtain rail (taking care to note that this may not be the same as the width of your window). Consult the table below matching the length of the rail to the width size, A-G. Single curtains may be ordered in A, C, E or G widths at half the price quoted per pair. The width of the single curtain is half that given below.

Rail widths up to:	cm ins	105 41	155 61	205 81	255 100	302 121	355 140	405 159
Double fullness pair of curtains	width	A	B	C	D	E	F	G

3. Measure the length of curtain needed from the point where you require the top of the curtain heading to be, to the point to which you require the curtain to hang. (Please note that the lengths quoted are for pricing purposes only, the curtains will be finished to the specific lengths given). For intermediate lengths, select the price of the next group up.

4. Complete the order form, entering:
i. Print/colourway by print code (e.g. S56), colourway, (e.g. Cream/Plum) and reference number (e.g. *003012*)..
ii. Width sizes A-G.
iii. Length in inches.

If ordering a single curtain:
i. Enter ½ under quantity.
ii. If frilled state on which side of the curtain the frill should be sewn.

BLINDS

1. Choose design and colourway from those shown in the print index on pages 116-125 of this catalog.

2. Measure the final width of the blind rail you require, whether the blind is to be fitted inside or outside a recess. If it is to go outside a recess an overlap of at least 9.5 cm each side is recommended. Please ensure that measurements are accurate.

3. Measure the length from the point where the top of the blind heading is to be to the point at which the bottom of the blind is required when fully lowered. Festoon blinds are made slightly longer than the given length to allow for the festoon effect. For intermediate lengths select the price of the blind the next size up.

4. Complete the order form, entering:
i. Print/colourway by print code (e.g. S56), colourway (e.g. Cream/Plum) and reference number (e.g. *003012*).
ii. Width in inches.
iii. Length in inches.

Cleaning instructions: We recommend dry cleaning for all curtains and blinds. Washing is possible but the unavoidable variation in the washing performance of the curtain, blind and lining fabrics may result in some differential shrinkage.

Delivery: As all items are individually finished by hand, six weeks is the usual time to allow for delivery.

CUSTOMER INFORMATION

Colour Matching:
Whilst every effort is made to ensure as close a match as possible, colours shown in Laura Ashley catalog may not be an exact reproduction of the original tones found on the products. It should also be noted that there may be slight variations in colour between each batch of material and, in particular, between two different types of product, e.g. wallpaper and country furnishing cotton.

Sizes:
All measurements quoted in this catalog are only approximate, and may vary slightly in some cases. Please allow 3-5% shrinkage on all our fabrics.

Design:
Although every effort is made to supply each product as it is shown in the catalog, some variation in design may be necessary.

Featured Products:
As far as possible, Laura Ashley products are used in the room sets and other photographs in the catalog. However, other products may have to be used from time to time to create a particular effect.

Instructions for Use:
May we draw attention to the importance of reading and following the instructions given on the care and use of Laura Ashley products in order to ensure full performance of and satisfaction with the merchandise.

Discontinuations:
The collection outlined in this catalog is intended to be available until December 1985. From November 1st, Laura Ashley shop staff and Customer Services Departments will be in a position to advise you of any references which are unlikely to be carried in the 1986 range of Home Decoration.

Stocking Policy:
As our shops are limited in space, some may not carry the full range in stock at any one time. However, all Laura Ashley furnishing shops and Postal Departments are normally able to take your personal order for any item in this collection.

Prices:
Whilst every effort is made to maintain the prices given in this catalog, unavoidable adjustments may occasionally take place. Shop staff, Postal Departments and Customer Services Departments will be pleased to advise you in the case of alterations.

Refunds:
We hope you will be fully satisfied with your purchases. However, should you have any cause for dissatisfaction, please, if possible, take the article in question, together with the receipt, to the original shop of purchase or contact the Customer Services address above. We regret that refunds cannot be made outside the country of original purchase.

Sales Taxes:
Laura Ashley has facilities for tax refunds where appropriate. Please enquire at the time of purchase.

General Information:
If you would like to receive advance information on our future collections and catalogs, require further information about our Mail Order service, or have any queries concerning an order which you have placed, please contact:
The Mail Order Department, Laura Ashley Inc.,
55 Triangle Boulevard., Carlstadt, New Jersey 07072.
For general enquiries, or, if you are at all dissatisfied with any service which you have received, please contact:
Laura Ashley Mail Order Customer Service Department,
55 Triangle Boulevard, Carlstadt. New Jersey 07072.

WALLPAPER CALCULATOR (Number of Rolls needed for walls)

Wall height from skirting in feet	Measurement round room in feet (inc. doors and windows): 33	36	39	43	46	49	52	56	59	62	66	69	72
6′6″ to 7′2″	5	5	5	6	6	7	7	7	8	8	9	9	10
7′2″ to 7′10″	5	5	6	6	7	7	8	8	9	9	10	10	10
7′10″ to 8′6″	5	6	6	7	7	8	8	9	9	10	10	11	11
8′6″ to 9′2″	6	6	7	7	8	8	9	9	10	11	11	12	12
9′2″ to 9′10″	6	7	7	8	8	9	9	10	11	11	12	12	13
9′10″ to 10′6″	6	7	8	8	9	10	10	11	11	12	13	13	14
10′6″ to 11′2″	7	7	8	9	9	10	11	11	12	13	13	14	15

FABRIC REPEAT (to nearest ½ inch.) Stripes & Plains have no repeats.

Please note: Recommended wallpaper repeat is 25 ins. for all designs.

Design	Repeat	Design	Repeat	Design	Repeat
Albert	3	Gingham	1	Polly	1
Antoinette	9	Grapes	4	Petite Fleur	3
Bembridge	2½	Hamilton	12½	Pondicherry	3½
Bindweed	3	Harbour	1	Poona	1½
Blue Ribbons	12½	Harebell	8	Q. Anne's Needlework	1
Campion	8½	Harriet	3	Rawalpindi	6
Clarissa	12½	Imogen	1½	Rectory Garden	2
Clifton Castle	8	Indienne	8	Rosamund	3
Clover	1½	Jaipur	5	Salon	6
Conservatory	6	Jessica	8½	Scottish Thistle	1
Convolvulous	7½	Joy	25	Sea Spray	1
Cordelia	12½	Kate	1½	Shepherd's Purse	8½
Cornflower	1½	Kew Gardens	25	Simla	1
Cottage Sprig	4	Lily of the Valley	8	Stipple	none
Cotton Seed	1	Malcolm	8	Stitchwort	½
Country Roses	1½	Mary Ann	4	Summertime	12½
Damask	25	Meadow Flowers	12	Sweet Briar	12½
Dandelion	6	Michaelmas	6	Tapestry	25
Deauville	6	Midsummer	25	Trefoil	1½
Delhi	4	Milfoil	3	Trellis	2
Edward	3	Ming	5	Tulips	8
Emma	12½	Morning Parlour	6	Venetia	25
Emmeline	25	Mr. Jones	2	White Bower	25
Emperor	25	Nutmeg	1	Wickerwork	1
English Garden	12½	Paisley	1	Wild Cherry	4
Favorita	25	Paisley Stripe	3	Wild Clematis	3½
Florentina	6	Palmetto	1	Wild Damson	1
Floribunda	6½	Penelope	1½	Wind Spray	8½
Fuchsias	5	Periwinkle	12½	Wood Violet	2½
Garlands	25				

COUNTRY FURNISHING COTTON CURTAINS Tie-backs $22.00 per pair

All prices are per pair. Finished Length up to:	WIDTH OF PLAIN CURTAIN					FRILLS
	A – 43″	B – 64″	C – 89″	D – 110″	W – 131″	ADD
48 ins	$109.00	$174.00	$231.00	$289.00	$325.00	$10.00
54 ins	$120.00	$193.00	$255.00	$319.00	$363.00	$11.50
60 ins	$130.00	$212.00	$280.00	$349.00	$402.00	$13.00
66 ins	$143.00	$230.00	$305.00	$381.00	$442.00	$14.50
72 ins	$155.00	$249.00	$330.00	$415.00	$481.00	$16.00
78 ins	$166.00	$268.00	$354.00	$443.00	$519.00	$17.50
84 ins	$177.00	$286.00	$379.00	$473.00	$557.00	$19.00
90 ins	$189.00	$306.00	$405.00	$506.00	$599.00	$20.50
96 ins	$201.00	$321.00	$430.00	$537.00	$638.00	$22.00
102 ins	$212.00	$342.00	$455.00	$567.00	$676.00	$23.50
108 ins	$224.00	$361.00	$479.00	$598.00	$715.00	$25.00
114 ins	$235.00	$381.00	$505.00	$631.00	$755.00	$26.50
120 ins	$248.00	$399.00	$530.00	$661.00	$794.00	$28.00

ROMAN SHADES : COUNTRY FURNISHING COTTON

FINISHED LENGTH	FINISHED WIDTH		
	21″	42″	59″
42 ins	$118.00	$154.00	$211.00
54 ins	$136.00	$176.00	$241.00
66 ins	$160.00	$204.00	$282.00
78 ins	$183.00	$235.00	$323.00
90 ins	$207.00	$264.00	$363.00
102 ins	$231.00	$293.00	$404.00
114 ins	$255.00	$322.00	$445.00
126 ins	$267.00	$336.00	$465.00

CHINTZ/DRAWING ROOM FABRIC CURTAINS Tie-backs $22.00 per pair

All prices are per pair. Finished Length up to:	WIDTH OF PLAIN CURTAIN					FRILLS
	A - 43″	B – 64″	C – 89″	D – 110″	W – 131″	ADD
48 ins	$137.00	$224.00	$307.00	$389.00	———	$12.00
54 ins	$152.00	$246.00	$339.00	$432.00	———	$13.50
60 ins	$165.00	$269.00	$371.00	$477.00	———	$15.00
66 ins	$180.00	$293.00	$406.00	$525.00	———	$16.50
72 ins	$195.00	$318.00	$439.00	$571.00	———	$18.00
78 ins	$209.00	$342.00	$471.00	$617.00	———	$19.50
84 ins	$223.00	$365.00	$504.00	$662.00	———	$21.00
90 ins	$239.00	$390.00	$539.00	$711.00	———	$22.50
96 ins	$254.00	$414.00	$573.00	$757.00	———	$24.00
102 ins	$268.00	$438.00	$605.00	$802.00	———	$25.50
108 ins	$282.00	$461.00	$638.00	$848.00	———	$27.00
114 ins	$298.00	$486.00	$673.00	$897.00	———	$28.50
120 ins	$312.00	$510.00	$705.00	$942.00	———	$30.00

ROMAN SHADES : CHINTZ & DRAWING ROOM FABRIC

FINISHED LENGTH	FINISHED WIDTH		
	21″	42″	59″
42 ins	$131.00	$170.00	$238.00
54 ins	$159.00	$194.00	$270.00
66 ins	$176.00	$226.00	$317.00
78 ins	$202.00	$259.00	$363.00
90 ins	$228.00	$291.00	$409.00
102 ins	$255.00	$323.00	$456.00
114 ins	$281.00	$356.00	$502.00
126 ins	$295.00	$372.00	$525.00

FESTOON BLINDS – COUNTRY FURNISHING COTTON

FINISHED LENGTH	FINISHED WIDTH					
	28″	39″	47″	52″	65″	71″
36 ins	$112.00	$124.00	$132.00	$182.00	$194.00	$201.00
42 ins	$125.00	$137.00	$145.00	$203.00	$215.00	$222.00
48 ins	$141.00	$151.00	$158.00	$222.00	$236.00	$242.00
54 ins	$153.00	$164.00	$173.00	$242.00	$256.00	$263.00
60 ins	$166.00	$178.00	$186.00	$263.00	$277.00	$284.00
66 ins	$180.00	$189.00	$198.00	$284.00	$297.00	$305.00
72 ins	$193.00	$205.00	$214.00	$305.00	$318.00	$325.00
78 ins	$206.00	$218.00	$227.00	$324.00	$339.00	$346.00
84 ins	$219.00	$233.00	$241.00	$345.00	$360.00	$367.00

FESTOON BLINDS – CHINTZ/DRAWING ROOM FABRIC

FINISHED LENGTH	FINISHED WIDTH					
	28″	39″	47″	52″	65″	71″
36 ins	$143.00	$157.00	$166.00	$229.00	$245.00	$252.00
42 ins	$159.00	$173.00	$183.00	$255.00	$271.00	$279.00
48 ins	$177.00	$191.00	$200.00	$281.00	$297.00	$305.00
54 ins	$207.00	$208.00	$218.00	$307.00	$324.00	$331.00
60 ins	$211.00	$226.00	$236.00	$334.00	$353.00	$358.00
66 ins	$228.00	$243.00	$253.00	$360.00	$377.00	$385.00
72 ins	$245.00	$261.00	$271.00	$386.00	$404.00	$412.00
78 ins	$262.00	$278.00	$288.00	$412.00	$430.00	$438.00
84 ins	$280.00	$296.00	$306.00	$439.00	$457.00	$465.00

U.S. SHOP ADDRESSES

New York 714 Madison Avenue, New York
New York 10021 212-371-0606
San Francisco 563 Sutter Street, San Francisco
California 94102 415-788-0190
San Francisco 1827 Union Street, San Francisco
California 94123 415-922-7200
Boston 83 Newbury Street, Boston
Massachusetts 02116 617-536-0505
Westport 85 Main Street, Westport
Connecticut 06880 203-226-7495
Washington 3213 M Street, NW, Georgetown
Washington D.C. 20007 202-338-5481
Chicago Watertower Place, 835 N. Michigan Avenue
Chicago, Illinois 60611 312-951-8004
Ardmore 29 Suburban Square, Ardmore
Pennsylvania 19003 215-896-0208
Atlanta Lenox Square, 3393 Peachtree Road, Atlanta
Georgia 30326 404-231-0685
Hackensack Riverside Square, Route 4 & Hackensack
Avenue, Hackensack, New Jersey 07601 201-488-0130
Costa Mesa 3333 Bristol Street, South Coast Plaza
Costa Mesa, California 92626 714-545-9322
Baltimore Pratt Street Pavilion, Harborplace
Baltimore, Maryland 21202 301-539-0500
Short Hills The Mall at Short Hills, Short Hills
New Jersey 07078 201-467-5657
Ft Lauderdale The Galleria at Ft Lauderdale, 2493 E.
Sunrise Blvd., Ft Lauderdale, Florida 33304 305-563-2300
Oakbrook 222-224 Oakbrook Center, Oakbrook
Illinois 60521 312-789-9195
Beachwood 203 Beachwood Place, 26300 Cedar Road
Beachwood, Ohio 44122 216-831-7621
Stamford 214 Stamford Town Center, Stamford
Connecticut 06902 203-324-1067
Houston Galleria 1, 5015 Westheimer Road, Houston
Texas 77056 713-871-9669

Century City Century City Shopping Center, 10250
Santa Monica Blvd., Los Angeles, CA 90067 213-553-0807
Dallas Dallas Galleria, & 13350 Dallas Parkway,
Dallas, Texas 75240 214-980-9858
Manhasset 2042 Northern Blvd., Americana Shopping
Center, Manhasset, New York 11030 516-365-4636
Seattle 405 University Street, Four Seasons Olympic
Hotel, Seattle Washington 98101 206-343-9637
Northbrook 2164 Northbrook Court, Northbrook
Illinois 60062 312-480-1660
St Louis 74 Plaza Frontenac, St. Louis
Missouri 63131 314-993-4410
Troy 2845 Somerset Mall, Troy
Michigan 48084 313-649-0890
Philadelphia 1721 Walnut Street, Philadelphia
Pennsylvania 19103 215-496-0492
Bullock's-Westwood 10861 Weyburn Avenue
Los Angeles, California 90024 213-208-4211 ext. 254
Bullock's-Pasadena 401 South Lake Avenue,
Pasadena California 91101 818-792-0211 ext. 265
Princeton 46 Nassau Street, Palmer Square, Princeton
New Jersey 08542 609-683-4760
Providence Davol Square Mall, Providence,
Rhode Island 02903 401-273-1120
Chestnut Hill The Mall at Chestnut Hill
Chestnut Hill, Massachusetts 02167 617-965-7640
Pittsburgh 20 Commerce Court, Station Square,
Pittsburgh, Pennsylvania 15219 412-391-7993
Palm Beach 320 Worth Avenue, Palm Beach
Florida 33480 305-832-3188
Minneapolis 208 City Center, 40 South 7th Street
Minneapolis, Minnesota 55402 612-332-6066
La Jolla 7852 Girard Avenue, La Jolla
California 92038 619-459-3733
Palo Alto Stanford Shopping Center, Palo Alto
California 94304 415-328-0560
New Orleans 151 Canal Place, New Orleans
Louisiana 70130 504-522-9403

Nashville The Mall at Green Hills, 2148 Abbot Martin
Road, Nashville, Tennessee 37215 615-383-0131
Walnut Creek 1171 Broadway Plaza, Walnut Creek
California 94596 415-947-5920
Kansas City 308 West 47th Street, Country Club Plaza,
Kansas City, Missouri 64112 816-931-0731
Burlington 23 Church Street, Burlington
Vermont 05401 802-658-5006
Williamsburg Merchants Square, Williamsburg
Virginia 23185 804-229-0353
Indianapolis Fashion Mall, 8702 Keystone Crossing
Indianapolis, Indiana 46240 317-848-9855
White Flint White Flint Mall, North Bethesda
Maryland 20895 301-984-3223
Boca Raton Town Center, 6000 West Glades Road,
Boca Raton, Florida 33432 305-368-5622
Tulsa Utica Square, 1846 E. 21st Street, Tulsa
Oklahoma 74114 918-749-5001
Denver 1439 Larimer Street, Denver
Colorado 80202 303-571-0050
Fairfax Fair Oaks Mall, Fairfax
Virginia 22033 703-352-7960
Beverly Center 121 N. Lacienega Blvd., Los Angeles
California 90048 213-854-0490
Richmond 1217 E. Cary Street, Richmond
Virginia 23219 804-644-1050
South Street Seaport 4 Fulton Street, New York
New York 10024
New York Westside 398 Columbus Avenue,
New York, New York 10024
Houston II 1000 West Oaks Mall, Houston
Texas 75082 713-496-3217
Dallas II North Park Center, Dallas
Texas 75225 214-369-8393
Hartford Westfarms Mall, Farmington,
Connecticut
Paramus Paramus Park, Route 17, Paramus, New Jersey
07652

HOW TO ORDER

Please read carefully before completing the order form.

1. To order you can toll free 1 – 800 – 367 – 2000, 24 hours a day, seven days a week. Or you can complete the attached order form and mail in the pre-addressed envelope to Laura Ashley Inc., Mail Order Department, 55 Triangle Boulevard, Carlstadt, New Jersey 07072. Please fill in the form as shown in the example. Product code numbers and descriptions can be found on the price list. Colourways and reference numbers are explained in the catalog guide, page 56.

2. Minimum fabric length supplied is one yard. Please order full yard lengths only. The table shows the maximum continuous lengths in which fabric can be supplied: Country Furnishing Cotton 35 yards, Chintz 25 yards, Upholstery Fabric 25 yards, Drawing Room Fabric 35 yards, Fabric Borders 20 yards, Plastic Coated Fabric 25 yards, Lining Fabric 50 yards.

3. Laura Ashley Gift Service. We will happily send items direct to a friend or relative. Complete the order form as usual, including the name and address of the person to whom we should send the goods.
Please check the box on the order form if you would like the gift wrap.

4. We aim to dispatch all goods within 14 days, but please allow 28 days delivery. We will inform you if, for any reason, we cannot send your order within this time. For information regarding your order we may be contacted at the number and address noted above. With any customer service problems note the name of the Laura Ashley Representative.

5. If any of our products do not meet your expectations, you can return them to us within 14 days, post paid and in good condition, and we will refund your original cost. We would be grateful if you could quote your order number upon return. We regret that refunds can only be made on Made to Measure Curtains and cut fabric if they are faulty or do not comply with your original order.

6. We aim to maintain prices throughout the year but reserve the right to change them without notice. We will inform you of price changes before shipping your order. All prices are listed on this page.

PRICE LIST

Please note that product numbers shown below should be quoted when ordering.

WALLPAPER (pages 56)

301	Wallpaper (per roll)	**$17.50**

FABRICS All fabrics are priced per yard

201	Country Furnishing Cotton (56)	**$12.00**
215	Drawing Room Fabric (page 80)	**$16.50**
208	Chintz (page 84)	**$15.50**
209	Upholstery Fabric (page 86)	**$23.50**
205	Plastic Coated Fabric (page 87)	**$17.00**
206	Lining Fabric (page 115)	**$4.50**

BORDERS (page 88)

210	Fabric Borders (2 ¼ in wide)	**$3.50**
	F510, L631, T210, F215, F274 & F46	
210	Fabric Borders (4 ¼ in wide)	**$4.50**
	F368, P897, F221, F512, F116, F539 & F45	
302	Wallpaper Borders (per pack)	**$6.50**

TRIMMINGS (page 92)

719	Gimp (per yard)	**$2.00**
718	Fringing (per yard)	**$4.00**
717	Tie-backs (per pair)	**$14.00**

PAINTS (page 94)

402	Gloss Paint (1 litre can)	**$16.50**
401	Emulsion Paint (2.5 litre can)	**$26.50**

CERAMIC TILES (page 96)

681	8 Inch Tiles (per tile)	**$4.00**
	Box of 25 Tiles (1 sq. yd.)	**$87.50**
686	6 Inch Tiles (per tile)	**$2.00**
	Box of 22 Tiles (½ sq. yd.)	**$37.50**

BORDER TILES (page 99)

688	Box of 25 Tile Borders	**$32.50**

LIGHTING (page 100)

576	Large Lampshade	**$36.00**
577	Medium Lampshade	**$31.00**
578	Small Lampshade	**$26.00**
571	Large Octagonal Lampbase	**$50.00**
573	Large Rounded Lampbase	**$42.50**
574	Medium Rounded Lampbase	**$36.50**
575	Small Rounded Lampbase	**$32.50**

DRESSING RM. COLLECTION (page 102)

561	Sponge Bag	**$19.50**
562	Cosmetic Bag	**$16.00**
559	Small Cosmetic Bag	**$13.50**
567	Sewing/Jewelry Box	**$32.50**
566	Sewing Kit	**$12.50**
568	Tissue Box & Cover	**$14.50**

DESK COLLECTION (page 103)

543	Small Square Frame	**$12.50**
541	Medium Single Frame	**$13.50**
542	Large Single Frame	**$17.50**
551	Double Folding Frame	**$14.50**
545	Desk Note Pad	**$15.00**
593	Refill for Note Pad	**$5.25**
553	Photo Album	**$32.50**
554	Refills for Photo Album	**$8.00**

DINING COLLECTION (page 104)

501	Square Tablecloth	**$22.00**
502	Rectangular Tablecloth	**$32.00**
	Small Round Tablecloth	**$32.00**
506	Round Tableclth	**$42.00**
503	Set of Four Napkins	**$16.00**
524	Place Mat	**$7.00**
522	Tea Cosy	**$16.50**
523	Egg Cosy	**$5.00**

CUSHIONS (page 106)

513	Round Frilled Cushion Cover	**$23.00**
	Round Frilled Cover with Pad	**$35.00**
512	Square Frilled Cushion Cover	**$23.00**
	Square Frilled Cover with Pad	**$35.00**
519	Round Pad	**$12.00**
518	Square Pad	**$12.00**
525	Piped Cushion Cover (Chintz)	**$21.00**
511	Columbine/Emma Cover	**$21.00**

PATCHWORK QUILTS (page 114)

601	Single Patchwork Quilt	**$195.00**
602	Double Patchwork Quilt	**$310.00**
608	Extra Large (call for prices)	

PATCHWORK PIECES (page 114)

674	Square Patchwork (per pack)	**$10.00**
680	Hexagonal P'work (per pack)	**$10.00**

LACE PANELS (page 115)

671	Lace Panels	**$50.00**

PUBLICATIONS (page 135)

	Seasonal Catalog	**$2.00**
913	A House in the Cotswolds	**$5.00**
662	LA Book of Home Decorating	**$24.95**

TAXES

We must collect taxes for the following localities as indicated on the chart. This applies to the delivery address.

State	Local Areas	Rate
CALIFORNIA	STATE	4.75%
	San Francisco	6.5%
	Orange	6.0%
	Los Angeles	6.5%
	La Jolla	6.0%
	Contra Costa	6.5%
	Santa Clara	6.5%
CONNECTICUT (Children's Garments are not taxed.)	ALL	7.5%
FLORIDA	ALL	5.0%
GEORGIA	STATE	3.00%
	Fulton	5.0%
ILLINOIS	STATE	4.0%
	Du Page	5.25%
	Chicago	7.0%
	Cook	6.0%
INDIANA	ALL	5.0%
LOUISIANA	STATE	3.0%
	Orleans Parish	8.0%
MARYLAND	ALL	5.0%
MASSACHUSETTS	ALL	5.0%
MICHIGAN	ALL	4.0%
MINNESOTA	ALL	6.0%
MISSOURI	STATE	4.125%
	St. Louis	5.625%
	Jackson/Clay	5.625%
	Pratt	5.625%
NEW JERSEY	ALL	6.0%
NEW YORK	STATE	4.0%
	NYC/Nassau	8.25%
OHIO	STATE	5.0%
	Cuyahoga	6.5%
OKLAHOMA	STATE	3.0%
	Tulsa	6.0%
PENNSYLVANIA	ALL	6.0%
RHODE ISLAND	ALL	6.0%
TENNESSEE	STATE	5.5%
	Nashville	7.75%
TEXAS	STATE	4.125%
	Harris	6.125%
	Dallas	6.125%
VERMONT	ALL	4.0%
VIRGINIA	STATE	3.0%
	Williamsburg	4.0%
	Richmond	4.0%
WASHINGTON	STATE	6.5%
	King	7.9%
WASHINGTON DC	ALL	6.0%
COLORADO	ALL	3.0%
	Denver	6.6%

LAURA ASHLEY — **Home Furnishings Order Form** — **1-800-367-2000**

Send your order with payment using the enclosed envelope, to:
Laura Ashley, 55 Triangle Blvd., Carlstadt, N.J. 07072 or call toll free 1-800-367-2000.

My address and phone is			Delivery address if different from that on left		
Mr/Mrs/Miss			Mr/Mrs/Miss		
Address			Address		
City	State	Zip	City	State	Zip
Phone			Phone		

211884

Please note Size applies to garments only. Design Number and Reference Number apply to Home Furnishings only.

Product Code No.	Size	Product Description	Reference Number	Design Number	Colourway	Quantity	Cost

Made to Measure Curtains & Festoon Blind Order Form (see price page for instructions on how to order & prices.)

Design Number	Colourway	Reference Number	Number of Pairs	Number of Blinds	Fabric CFC, DRF & Chintz	Length	Fabric	Curtains Plain or Frilled	Curtain Tie-backs

Sofa and Armchair

Design Number	Fabric Upholstery CFC, DRF or Chintz only	Reference Number	Design Number	Colourway	Valance: gathered, straight, or box pleat?	Colour of Piping (CFC only)	Quantity	Unit Price	Total Price

Shipping Charges: If your zip code begins with: 010-299 you pay $5.00. — Add Local Tax
(There is only one price per order) 300-499 you pay $5.50. — Add Shipping
500-994 you pay $6.00. — GRAND TOTAL

I'll pay by: Check/Money Order ☐ Visa☐ Master Card ☐ American Express ☐ Check Box for Gift Wrap ☐

My Card Number is Exp. Date Signed

Make check payable to "Laura Ashley Inc."

TAXES: We must collect taxes for the following localities as indicated on the chart. This applies to the delivery address.

State	Local Areas	Rate
CALIFORNIA	STATE	4.75%
	San Francisco	6.5%
	Orange	6.0%
	Los Angeles	6.5%
	La Jolla	6.0%
	Contra Costa/Santa Clara	6.5%
COLORADO	STATE	3.0%
	Denver	6.6%
CONNECTICUT	ALL	7.5%
WASHINGTON, D.C.	ALL	6.0%
VERMONT	ALL	4%
FLORIDA	ALL	5.0%
GEORGIA	STATE	3.0%
	Fulton	3.0%
ILLINOIS	STATE	4.0%
	Du Page	5.25%
	Chicago	7.0%
	Cook	6.0%
MARYLAND	ALL	5.0%
MASSACHUSETTS	ALL	5.0%
MICHIGAN	ALL	4.0%
MINNESOTA	ALL	6.0%
MISSOURI	STATE	4.125%
	St. Louis	5.625%
	Jackson/Clay/Pratt	5.625%
NEW JERSEY	ALL	6.0%
NEW YORK	STATE	4.0%
	NYC/Nassau	8.25%
OHIO	STATE	5.0%
	Cuyahoga	6.5%
PENNSYLVANIA	ALL	6.0%
RHODE ISLAND	ALL	6.0%
TENNESSEE	STATE	5.5%
	Nashville	7.75%
TEXAS	STATE	4.125%
	Harris	6.125%
	Dallas	6.125%
WASHINGTON	STATE	6.5%
	King	7.9%
VIRGINIA	STATE	3.0%
	Williamsburg	4.0%
	Fairfax	4.0%
INDIANA	ALL	5.0%
LOUISIANA	STATE	3.0%
	Orleans Parish	8.0%
OKLAHOMA	STATE	3.0%
	Tulsa	6.0%